FEAST!

CANADIAN NATIVE CUISINE
FOR ALL SEASONS

ANDREW GEORGE JR. AND ROBERT GAIRNS

Doubleday Canada Limited

Toronto New York London Sydney Auckland

Canadian Cataloguing in Publication Data

George, Andrew

    Feast! canadian native cuisine for all seasons

Includes Index.

ISBN 0-385-25580-2

1. Indian cookery. 2. Cookery, Canadian - British Columbia style.
3. Indians of North America - Northwest, Pacific - Food.
I. Gairns, Robert. II. Title.

TX715.6.G46. 1996   641.59'2970711   C96-930577-X

Design and page composition by Joseph Gisini / Andrew Smith Graphics, Inc.

Native art references supplied by Warner Naziel

Food photography by Ross Durant

Food styling by Nathan Fong

Background props by Ross Durant

Prop styling by Karen Heaps

Additional prop styling by Valerie Bedwell

Assistants: Nic Lehoux and Greg Shurmann

Printed and bound in Canada

Published in Canada by
Doubleday Canada Limited
105 Bond Street
Toronto, Ontario
Canada M5B 1Y3

For my parents Rita George (Gihl Lakh Khun) and Andrew George Sr. (Tsaibesa).
To my wife and daughter, Cecelia and McKayla Brazeau-George.
For my brothers and sisters Betty, Brian, Gary, Cindy, Greg and Corinne.
In memory of my grandparents, Thomas George (Gisdewe) and Mary George (Tsaibesa)
and my mother's parents, Julie Isaac (Nu'yak oohn) and Paddy Isaac (Satson).
Also dedicated to the rest of the George family
and the Hereditary Chiefs of the Wet'suwet'en people.

— Andrew George Jr.

◈

For my Jeannie, Jamie and Karen.
For our little one — Siobhan 'Piquette.'
For all those who came before us and all those who will come after us.
For Sandy, and my mother "Mame."

— Robert Gairns

CONTENTS

So'h ga nec kewh dalht! Have a good meal!

BOOK ONE

INTRODUCTION

THE OLYMPIC JOURNEY OF ANDREW GEORGE JR.

Told by Robert Gairns and Andrew George Jr.

If Andrew George Jr. had catered the very first Olympic Games, chances are he would have used many of the same ingredients he works with today, a mere 2,773 years later — for as old as they might be, even the original Olympics are newcomers, Aboriginally-speaking. Andrew's people — the Wet'suwet'en Nation — hunted, fished and gathered the bounties of Mother Earth in Now'h Yin'h Ta'h, their traditional territory, thousands of years before Homer composed the *Iliad* and the *Odyssey,* Rome was founded or the Chou Dynasty flourished, thousands of years before the first Olympic Games were a glimmer in their founder's eye.

Less likely is that he would have named a dish back then *savarin de lièvre ou de lapin au sang de mûres et aux canneberges*, which is culinary-speak for rabbit with two berry sauces. Even the most exotic meal he prepares today does not carry such a grand appellation, and yet an Andrew George culinary creation could delight the palate of the most discriminating gourmet in the world. And has.

The Olympics began on the Plains of Olympia in 776 B.C. to honour Zeus, the supreme god of the ancient Greeks. Not only were there the athletic contests associated with the modern games but also — Greece being the cradle of civilization — poetry and music were integral to the event. And what, after all, would these things have been without food and drink, the nourishment and the inspiration for body and soul?

Gisdewe, the late Thomas George, a Hereditary Chief of the Bear Clan (Git dum den), and Tsaibesa, the late Mary George of the Killer Whale Clan (Hiksulu), are grandparents of Andrew Jr. His parents, Rita and Andrew Sr., who inherited his mother's traditional name, raised six children at Toody Ni ("Where the Hill Faces the River") in central interior British Columbia. Through matrilineal descendancy Andrew Jr. — the third-born of his mother, Chief Gihl Lakh Khun — is a member of the Bear Clan. He too is in line to become a Hereditary Chief.

It is in this land and in these proud and resourceful people — all those who have gone before and all those yet to be born into the Wet'suwet'en

Nation — that the inspiration, courage and determination of Andrew George Jr. have their roots. They are qualities he has had to summon on more than one occasion in the little more than thirty years he has been on this earth. They define and embody the character of the quiet, unassuming, gentle young man, and have guided him on his journey.

What today's younger generation would imagine to be a deprived existence, Andrew reflects on with fondness and affection as a good and simple life. A small house with no running water nonetheless was a warm and loving home nestled in a verdant, abundant valley in one of the most breathtakingly beautiful places on earth, known as the Bulkley Valley.

I am a proud mother of six children. We have four boys and two girls. I am very proud to see each one of my children succeed in their chosen fields. They have all graduated from high school and have successfully completed their post-secondary education.

I am a strong believer in our Wet'suwet'en culture and customs, and the use of natural resources such as the harvesting and preservation of salmon, hunting, berry picking and gathering our natural herbs and medicines from the land.

This is what Aboriginal rights involve, and our lives are governed in the Feast Hall. The hereditary system of the Wet'suwet'en is based on maternal lineage, which means the children follow the mother's clan. I am part of the Bear Clan (Git dum den), so my children are also in the Bear Clan.

The other clans in the Wet'suwet'en system are Killer Whale (Lahk-sam us-u), Caribou (Lahk-seehl-u), Beaver (Tsa-u) and Frog (Gihl-tse-u). The land and resources are divided according to the clan system and are governed and protected by each individual clan through the potlatch system.

Because we live off the land we must also protect the land. This is where we taught our children to be self-dependent. One, the third eldest, became a chef. I taught them all how to cook at a very young age. At the age of fifteen Andy was hired by a mining company as a camp cook. He knew how to cook in a camp because of his experience in the bush with his parents.

I can remember one Remembrance Day weekend when my husband and myself decided to sleep in. Andy Jr. came into the bedroom with a plateful of spaghetti and sauce he had just prepared. He proudly stood by our bed holding the plate in the palm of his hand like a waiter. When I reached up and tipped the plate to see what was on it, the spaghetti and sauce slid off onto my husband's face. I could not help but laugh because my husband ran toward the sink with spaghetti hanging all over him, even around his ears. Every now and then when we have spaghetti dinners, we all laugh about that incident.

RITA GEORGE (GIHL LAKH KHUN)

Season after season, year after year, these brothers and sisters of the bear and the killer whale went out on the land to share in its bounties, to re-establish their personal relationship with it and to respect the lessons it offers — for the land is life. It is the learning path, with no beginning and no end. It is forever.

> *When Mother Earth slipped into her soft robe of white there were fish to be caught through the ice, rabbits to be snared and grouse to be hunted.*
>
> *It was good too that the laughter carried well, across the frozen lake and through the still winter bush.*
>
> *In the freshness of early spring there were furs to be harvested and more fish to be taken from the mirror-clear, icy-cold lakes and rivers.*
>
> *In summer the salmon were to be canned or smoked, the rich, red succulent salmon that is a staple of the First Nations of the Pacific Northwest, and a much-prized delicacy with gourmets the world over.*
>
> *And as the days became warmer and warmer and the sun brighter and brighter, there were berries to be picked — juicy huckleberries and blueberries bursting with ripeness, leaving telltale signs around the children's mouths as they filled their baskets to overflowing.*
>
> *When once again the breath could be seen in the chill air, great care would be taken to walk softly, for underfoot the fallen autumn leaves and twigs lay anxious to signal the moose and the deer of the oncoming hunter.*
>
> *After all, Mother Earth must be fair to all her children.*

A time and a place where values supersede possessions, where fulfilment is measured more by what is done than by what is owned, where life is good because Mother Earth is generous and the Great Spirit is a wise teacher.

It is a life that Andrew must return to often.

> Such a magical thing, Tsaibesa's wood stove. Under her gentle, deft guidance it had powers. Of warmth. Of comfort. Of healing. Of imagination. Of fulfilment. Of joy.
>
> They were a team, Mary George and her large cast-iron friend. They were inseparable, and together they worked wonders transforming the gifts from Mother Earth into hot, delicious meals to place before an adoring and happy family around the kitchen table.
>
> As she kneaded and rolled the dough over and over into a smooth ball, a pair of tiny hands would eagerly join in the daily ritual. Standing on a chair beside Tsaibesa, flour and dough from head to foot, was five-year-old Andrew George Jr.
>
> He was helping Grandma make bannock.
>
> Every chance he could.

The 26-mile marathon is not for the faint of heart or the weak of will.

It is perhaps the most famous and certainly the most gruelling of all Olympic events. The marathon also is irrefutable evidence that Greek civilization condoned cruel and unusual punishment. To finish it, let alone place in the top three, is worthy of high praise, and perhaps a little therapy.

> All the best runners in town were at the starting line, anxious to please, to impress the girls, to win on this summer day in 1982. Not all were quite as excited about competing against an Indian.
>
> This would be yet another good test for a young man, a Wet'suwet'en who just could not quit, could not give up at anything, no matter what. It is the way of the Bear in the tradition of his people.
>
> The last year of high school, and then college was the next step. The discipline of the run would be good for his education. It is important to keep one's eyes on the dream.

For all the problems it would present, it was worth the year-long wait to get into the cook-training program at Vancouver Vocational Institute. Besides, there was always the memory of the second-place finish in the high-school marathon to think about when things got tough.

Like the fabled race, school in the big city was not going to be easy. It was large and strange and intimidating, and about two and a half hours on foot from Andrew's rooming house.

The 1984 Vancouver bus strike did little to make the learning path any easier for a frightened young man embarking on a three-term curriculum. Neither did the taunts from some fellow students that "Indians can't cook," and others who questioned his right to be there. Some still do.

The faculty suggested he drop out and return the next year, when the strike surely would be over. His response was typical of the young man. He walked the walk.

The money he earned as a part-time cook at the Vancouver Indian Friendship Centre helped pay for his schooling, and in 1985 Andrew George Jr. graduated. It was now official: he was a cook, a Wet'suwet'en cook who had proven his right to be wherever his talent, courage and determination would take him.

That would be far, but he did not know exactly how far. Who can say at such a young age?

His journey was just beginning.

Vancouver's Quilicum restaurant was unique. It was fashioned after the interior of a Haida house. The decor was rustic Pacific Northwest, cool and subdued. Its menu was strictly Aboriginal. It was also a place where visiting movie stars, musicians and other celebrities, even politicians, congregated when they were in town.

The Quilicum is where Andrew learned to cook professionally on a wood-burning grill and to prepare many Native dishes characteristic of the Pacific Northwest — wood-barbecued salmon, oysters, rabbit, caribou, smoked eulachons, steamed smoked Alaska black cod, crab in the shell, wild rice, seaweed and rice, crisp watercress salad, whipped soapalillie, cold raspberry soup.

There would be even more knowledge to be gained. That is the way of it for a young cook who aspires to be a world-class chef, a Wet'suwet'en who knows the learning path never ends.

Apprenticeship in the culinary craft is valued; in fact, it is a prerequisite for anyone aspiring to a career as a chef. Andrew combined more college training with fieldwork. While taking the apprenticeship programs at the British Columbia Institute of Technology, he was head cook for the First Nations Restaurant at Vancouver's Expo '86, where he received an Award of Excellence, and he honed his skills at the Avenue Grill on Vancouver's west side, completing the cycle at trendy Isadora's restaurant on Granville Island in 1988.

He was also learning something of the language of cooking. It came in handy, especially when he was hired as a cook at CP Hotels' new Château Whistler Resort in 1989, and then at Vancouver's Four Seasons Hotel, preparing banquets and working the garde manger, or meat locker.

> *This cooking business, it keeps you moving all the time. In the extreme heat and tension of the kitchen there is much noise and yelling always. Tsaibesa would not understand this. Her kitchen was a place of happiness and peace. It is important to keep centred. Never let it get to you. It is just the nature of this creative, temperamental profession. "Tsaibesa! Wood stove! Bannock! Now'h Yin'h Ta'h! Stay with me!"*

Part of the dream was to open his own restaurant, a first-class restaurant featuring the foods of the Aboriginal peoples of Canada's Pacific Northwest. Of course there would be room on the menu for Native foods from other parts of Canada too.

Almost a year's planning and hard work, raising money without government help. Finding a place and transforming it into the Toody Ni Grill and Catering Company in the Native Friendship centre on not-always-friendly East Hastings Street in downtown Vancouver.

Tsaibesa would be happy about this, and so would Gisdewe. Andrew Sr. and Rita certainly were as proud as parents could possibly be.

> *Andy Junior is a child of the Hereditary Chiefs who hold large trapping territories, called Now'h Yin'h Ta'h, which in our language means "keepers of the land." The traditional Wet'suwet'en territories are presently under land claims negotiations with the federal and provincial governments.*
>
> *As a father I have always been proud of Andy Jr. As we watched him grow older and progress he became a wise young man.*

He always liked to go out with us on the trapping
territory to hunt and trap beaver and other game animals.

My wife, Rita, and myself know a lot about our culture
and how to survive and we passed this knowledge on to our
children. This I believe is where Andy Jr. learned very well. He
is still a young man and has a long way to go in his career. We
are very proud of his accomplishments, and wherever he goes
and whatever he does, we as parents are very confident he has
the knowledge to make it.

Andy Jr. achieved his goal as a chef with his very own
initiative, just like the rest of our children.

Our children obtained their goals the hard way and in the
process learned about life. That is why I am very proud of
them and I want a brighter future for all our children.

ANDREW GEORGE SR. (TSAIBESA)

It was a grand opening, that summer day in 1991, and the gymnasium
of the Friendship Centre was big enough to hold all the guests and the
speakers, drummers and dancers, and still there was plenty of room for
all the children to run around the floor and dance and play.

The platters kept coming, for truly this was a feast that featured Native
cuisine with a Pacific Northwest flavour.

And after the sumptuous meal there was much praise to be offered and
thanks to be given for the journey of Andrew George Jr.

The Kwakiutl and Gitskan-Wet'suwet'en dancers, resplendent in their
striking black and red and white button blankets, danced and paid tribute
with their special songs. So did the Red Plume dancers and drummers in
the feathers and bustles and jingles typical of Prairie First Nations
traditional clothing, who performed the Grass Dance and the spectacular
Hoop dance as the grand finale to the evening.

A little piece of "Where the Hill Faces the River" had been brought to
Vancouver to be shared with all who would pass through the doors of
Toody Ni.

The restaurant, the catering business, coaching the softball team. So
much hard work, so many headaches, so many customers from all over
the world, it seemed, so many people and problems to deal with. But also
many favourable comments. So much fun, so rewarding. It was good to be
off to such a promising start, including being nominated for the Federal

Business Development Bank's Entrepreneur of the Year award.

Still, the last thing a chef needs in the always too busy middle of preparing a meal for his guests is to be called to the telephone. It is not a welcome interruption and usually invites a colourful reply from any kitchen conductor orchestrating the metamorphosis from menu to plate.

But this call! From out of nowhere!

Huh'di sowet'zen! Hello, how are you!

It all started in 1991, a year Robert Gairns and I will never forget. Early in the year I was lucky enough to get the call to be a member of the newly-formed Canadian Native Haute Cuisine Team, and was told we would be going to Frankfurt in October to compete against about 13,000 chefs from more than fifty countries at the World Culinary Olympics.

When Oudeheemin, the company organizing the team, was looking for candidates, they found me through the "Moccasin Telegraph," our Native gossip hotline. It was exciting news for a young man from the central interior of British Columbia — or anywhere, I would imagine. From my grandmother Tsaibesa's kitchen, to bush camp cook, to college, apprenticeship and then opening my Toody Ni Grill and Catering Company in Vancouver in only a few years — and now the Olympics! I'm not sure my head stopped spinning the whole year.

I was still trying to make a go of it with Toody Ni and the catering operation. Business was picking up as our name and good reviews got around. On any given day you would swear you were in the United Nations, with all the tourists and locals coming in for lunch and dinner.

At the same time I had to begin an intensive six-month training program for the Olympics. Chef Georges Chauvet was our amazing team manager. He's one of the superstars of our profession. He was manager for the gold-medal Canadian national culinary teams and has won more awards than anyone I know. He soon had us hitting the books pretty hard, and of course there was the hands-on training at the Sutton Place Hotel in Toronto under Chef Chauvet and Chef Niels Kjeldsen. None of us — Arnold Olson, a Cree from Saskatchewan; Bryan Sappier, a Micmac/Malecite from New Brunswick; Bertha Skye, a Cree married to a Cayuga from Six Nations of the Grand River, Ontario; David Wolfman, the Sto:lo from the interior of B.C., but living in Toronto, and me, the Wet'suwet'en from British Columbia — had ever faced the intense pressures of competing against so many outstanding chefs from around the world, and most of us considered the invitation to participate reward enough. But Chef Chauvet, a demanding yet loving taskmaster, reinforced our personal desire to work hard, to do our best. He gave us reason to believe we really had the talent to go for the gold.

In Olympic culinary competition, just like in the other Olympics, excellence in both individual skill and team performance is everything. There is no room for error, not against that calibre of world-class competition. Everything has to move with military precision — but with artistic creativity. And Chef Chauvet made us practice until our fingers and our backs ached and our minds were filled with things to remember. There were manuals to be studied, recipes to be learned, techniques to be mastered. Old fears to be conquered. "No, not good enough. Try again," Chef Chauvet would say. We all wanted to please him, to do it right. We followed the master and did it over and over again, until we were beginning to get it a little more right each time. We were also beginning to understand a tiny bit of what we were going to be up against in October.

The days flew by and we were finally on countdown to Frankfurt, Germany. Everybody was so busy getting ready for the trip and trying to get their own business in order — bills to pay, orders to place, staff to worry about — that we barely had time to think about the actual competitions. Then there was the checklist of what to take to Frankfurt. We had to make sure we had the traditional Native clothing we would be wearing when we were not in competition, and the Native artifacts we would be displaying in front of our tipi at the convention hall. And of course we packed our new chef's whites with the Canadian Native Haute Cuisine Team crest that we were so proud of. It was almost like organizing an army to go into battle. And none of it would have been possible without the energy and dedication of two remarkable people, Danielle Medina and Albert Diamond, who started Oudeheemin, who had the dream of forming a Canadian Native team to compete at the World Culinary Olympics, and who actually made it happen.

Robert was the writer and communications advisor for the Native Haute Cuisine Team, and over the months we had talked a lot on the phone. But we only got to meet each other at the first team briefing and press conference in Toronto. We have since become like brothers. Funny how fate sometimes has a way of bringing people together.

Somehow we managed to show up at the airport at the right time and on the right day. With all the bodies and assorted paraphernalia we were bringing, it was quite a sight: suitcases and war bonnets, drums and feathers, buckskins and moccasins. People at the airport must have thought we were heading off to shoot the sequel to *Dances with Wolves*.

We arrived in Frankfurt at six-thirty in the morning of Saturday, October 10, and on Sunday night we started. We were in the regional category of competition and were entered for events as individuals on five separate days. Normally a regional team does not compete in so many events, but perhaps Chef Chauvet was trying to make a point that we were not just one-shot wonders. Our entries — each a seven-course meal — were structured around the regions of the country, and each of us took a turn being the principal chef, while the rest acted as sous-chefs. Day one featured Native foods of the Atlantic provinces, day two the foods of the North, day three the foods of Quebec, day four the foods of Ontario, and finally day five — my turn as principal competitor — the foods of Western Canada.

Our participation in the competitions was not judged on taste. It didn't have anything to do with whose pastry was flakier or whose sauce was zestier. With thousands of world-class professional chefs from all over the globe offering diverse international cuisine, it would be impossible to fairly critique a presentation with the tastebuds. In this competitive pressure cooker on the world stage, it's all about the other kind of taste — presentation, imagination and artistic impression.

Each morning after an all-night session of preparing platters for presentation to the judges, we five Canadian Native chefs, dressed in our traditional clothing, or still sometimes in our chef's whites, would make ourselves available to the public. It was important to us to greet the thousands of people who crowded around our tipi and display of artifacts. After all, we were representing our Nations and our country. It was a matter of pride and honour and duty to do well. This was a routine to be repeated for five days with very little sleep. But if exhaustion set in it was not evident. Adrenalin is quite the elixir. And always we could slip inside the tipi, where it was dark and quiet, and the din outside was reduced to a faint murmur. A place of peace where one could think of family and friends and home, and Toody Ni. It was where the team would gather each day to purify ourselves with smoking sage and sweetgrass, to give thanks to the Creator for this honour.

The hall where the medals were presented was packed with people when the ceremonies took place late in the afternoon following each day's competitions — the international judges on the stage, and in the audience hundreds of chefs from other countries, and the international news media.

By the fifth day the Canadian Native Haute Cuisine Team had already won a fistful of medals — gold, silver and bronze — and there was a chance for more on this last day of competition. We had already more than accomplished our mission at Frankfurt. Just being selected to be there was special, and then to have won as many medals as we had was icing on the cake. But still, deep down inside, I wanted to win this one badly — for the Wet'suwet'en, for my family, for Native people, for my country and yes, for myself. Maybe I was still thinking of my second-place finish in my high school marathon a few years earlier, or maybe it was simply a case of getting caught up in the spirit of Olympic competition. I wanted to go for the gold one more time.

My menu that day:

Terrine of Smoked Fish
Beaver Tail Soup
Arrangement of Pacific Prawns
Smoked Arctic Char
Venison Tenderloin
Scallop Plate
Poached Pear

The pièce de résistance of the presentation was our chocolate sculpture that adorned the table. It was definitely a Pacific Northwest theme — a bear lying on its back with a salmon clutched in its front paws, above it an eagle swooping down to steal the salmon. It's a scene I had often seen before back home in British Columbia — but not in glazed chocolate.

We all waited breathlessly to find out who had won what. I'd bet there were more crossed fingers than at a liars' convention.

"Gold!" the judges announced. "Das Kanadische Team Eingeborener Koche!" And again, "Gold! Das Kanadische Team Eingeborener Koche!" The applause was thunderous.

The Canadian Native Haute Cuisine Team had won seven gold medals. And two silver and two bronze. Eleven medals in all!

To think we were the first Aboriginal team from anywhere in the world to have entered the competitions, and then to have won eleven medals! The bonus, of course, was that Canada's National Team won first place overall and the grand gold medal once again, and other Canadian regional teams won medals too. All this in a year when everyone agreed that the judging at Frankfurt was the toughest in the ninety-two-year history of the World Culinary Olympics. The Native team had surpassed all expectations, including our own. It just doesn't get much better than this.

In the end it was the "uniqueness, creativity and honest simplicity" of our team's platters that captured the respect and admiration of the judges. And the thousands of discerning visitors who saw the creations so beautifully displayed were awestruck at what Canada's Native team could do with moose, caribou, salmon, Arctic char, wild berries and all the other ingredients indigenous to our country.

I have been privileged to walk along a path where few others will set foot. In the tradition of my people I now have the obligation and the honour to share my good fortune. That is why I have spent so much time travelling to talk with young Native children and students over the past three years, encouraging them to go for the gold in their own lives, regardless of the career path they choose.

It is also why Robert and I have written *Feast!* as something more than a standard cookbook. We hope that you the reader will gain a little more insight into the cultures and traditions of Aboriginal peoples throughout Canada, expressed from the Wet'suwet'en heart.

The recipes and menus are ones I created over the years. As you will see, there is a strong Pacific Northwest Native flavour to most of them, but I have also been influenced by traditional Native recipes from all regions of Canada.

Feast! is about friendship, and sharing, and enjoyment, and love among the creatures of Mother Earth. Robert and I hope you will feel the same way after you have joined us on our journey through these pages.

MISS'IE. THANK YOU. MEEGWETCH.
ANDREW GEORGE JR. AND ROBERT GAIRNS

WET'SUWET'EN
THE FIRST PEOPLE OF THE VALLEY

*A*ndrew's people, part of the Carrier Nation, are known as the Wet'suwet'en, "the first people of the valley." They are among more than twenty First Nations peoples who live in what is now known as British Columbia.

Many would like to boast of having "discovered" this land of such incredible beauty, and some have. Even Buddhist monk explorers, according to the Imperial Library in Beijing, claimed to have discovered British Columbia in A.D. 449. If they did reach the west coast shores way back when, it is not nearly way back when enough to predate the Native cultures of the region — a compelling reason for them to be counted among the First Nations peoples of Canada.

The Wet'suwet'en are not coastal peoples, as are the Haida, the Tsimshian, the Nootka and the Kwakiutl. For thousands of years they have lived in the central interior of British Columbia — Ki, Kuz, Moricetown (Kya'h wiget) and Hagwilget. Their traditional territory includes the Skeena and Fraser watersheds — the migratory rivers for the Pacific salmon. It is a land that abounds with an incredible variety of flora and fauna that has sustained the Aboriginal peoples of the region.

The Wet'suwet'en come within the Athapaskan linguistic group, Aboriginal peoples living predominantly in British Columbia, Yukon and the Northwest Territories, but also scattered throughout Alberta, Saskatchewan and into northern Manitoba. The Athapaskan group covers an immense amount of real estate in the largest country on earth. It is also the largest Aboriginal linguistic group in Canada. It includes the Beaver, Carrier, Chilcotin, Chipewyan, Dogrib, Han, Hare, Kaska, Kutchin, Sarcee, Sekani, Slave, Tagish, Tahltan and Tutchone.

The Wet'suwet'en way of life is characterized by respect, balance and sharing between all creatures and all things, for in the eyes of the Creator they are all expected to live in harmony on Mother Earth.

Like other Aboriginal peoples of the Pacific Northwest, the Wet'suwet'en are divided into tribal groups and kinship units known as clans and houses. The clan system represents a set of beliefs and a relationship to the spirit of another being, such as the bear, the killer whale, the beaver, the grouse, the frog or the fireweed.

Clans have Hereditary Chiefs, who have been given special names that have been passed on from generation to generation, usually from the mother or the mother's brother, but it is not a title that is easily obtained. It must be earned by strength of character and exemplary deeds. Andrew George Sr. earned his mother's name, Tsaibesa, and the title of Hereditary Chief in this way, and Andrew Jr. will do the same. Each clan is led by one Hereditary High Chief, whose name is bestowed only upon those who demonstrate extraordinary knowledge, wisdom, leadership and vision, as agreed to by consensus in the Feast Hall.

FEAST! BA'LA'LAHTS

This book is named after the Wet'suwet'en feast, *denii ne'aas,* which means "people coming together." It is an appropriate title for a book that is not only about delicious things to eat but also about the ways of a people, the spirit and strength of character that have enabled the Wet'suwet'en to survive for thousands of years, as exemplified so perfectly by the George family.

As with other Aboriginal peoples of the Pacific Northwest, a feast or potlatch is much more than just people coming together to share food. It is the defining ceremony of Wet'suwet'en culture — the forum where important matters are discussed and where consensus is reached and witnessed by the people in the Feast Hall. Such matters could include such things as bestowing titles and rights to hunting, fishing and trapping territories, or settling disputes among parties. Everyone in the Feast Hall contributes to the decisions reached, and after an issue has been thoroughly deliberated upon, the point eventually is reached when the down from an eagle is sprinkled around, signifying that the matter is closed.

The mutually respectful, nonconfrontational nature of the feast helps make Wet'suwet'en society function smoothly and democratically. It also performs the function of a kind of living archives, whereby Wet'suwet'en history is passed on in the oral tradition of Aboriginal peoples.

Today a Feast Hall is usually the community centre, but in the old days it was a special long house in Wet'suwet'en communities.

A feast can be called for various purposes, usually by the Head Chief of a host clan, or in some cases by a person who carries a name. Since the homeland of the Wet'suwet'en is divided into traditional clan territories, an all-clan feast may be called to resolve questions of ownership or matters relating to territorial boundaries.

The most important gatherings are the funeral feast and the headstone feast. These are when names, titles and ownership are transferred to the living. An awarded name differs from a birth name in that it is passed on from a deceased name-holder only after a person has displayed qualities of goodness and honour in life, and only after everyone agrees that the candidate warrants such a tribute. A name is also a responsibility to be nourished and cared for, until such time as it is ready once again to be passed on to a new guardian, because it is associated with the name and reputation of a clan, and its territorial ownership.

When a name-holder passes away, a smoke party is held, where people are hired to take care of the funeral arrangements.

At a funeral feast of a name-holder two important functions take place. One is the communal grieving at the Feast Hall that helps ease the pain of the family and close friends of the person who has passed away. Also, if there is a suitable candidate, the recipient of the deceased's name is announced. Then, about a year later, the name, title and territory of the deceased are passed on at a headstone feast. At this feast, money is collected to pay for the funeral costs and debts the deceased may have incurred. It is also an occasion where gifts of appreciation are given to those who participated in the work involved in conducting the funeral.

Upon receiving a name at a headstone feast (*kan gu*), the recipient must act out in dance and song the name he or she has been awarded. During the ceremony the new chief will be given button blankets, drums, rattles and other regalia bearing the clan crest. The person receiving the name of a Hereditary High Chief will also receive a totem pole representative of the clans over which he or she has been granted guardianship.

For whatever reason it is called, a feast is usually presided over by a Hereditary High Chief and follows the same general pattern. The host clan issues invitations in person, through second parties or through the news media in the area. Guests gather outside the Feast Hall and, as they are announced, they are taken to their seats by a member of the host clan who knows the names and titles of the guests, and is well versed in the protocol of the occasion.

The Feast Hall is arranged with the host clan's table at the centre and invited clans on long tables on three of the four sides of the hall. The High Chiefs sit at the middle of the long tables, backs to the wall, facing the host table. Their heirs sit across from them, and other clan chiefs and guests sit on either side of them.

The ceremony begins with a prayer and a warm welcome by the host clan. Following an abundant meal featuring salmon, seasonal wild game, bannock, berries, tea and coffee, the business of the feast is conducted. It includes statements by the hosts who have called the feast, and responses by the invited chiefs. Mutual respects are paid among the chiefs as the business at hand is conducted. Gifts are given to the guests, and may include such items as blankets, food, tools and clothing. It is through the giving of gifts that the importance of the guests at the feast is recognized and their role as witnesses to the deliberations is appreciated in a tangible way. It is also important that guests accept their gifts to demonstrate appreciation for the hospitality offered. The Wet'suwet'en and other Aboriginal peoples of the Pacific Northwest are generous givers and grateful receivers.

Prayers and thanks are offered to conclude the ceremonies, and another feast comes to a close. And so the circle of Wet'suwet'en life continues.

THE SALMON HARVEST

The story of Aboriginal peoples in the Pacific Northwest, whether coastal or inland inhabitants, would be incomplete without reference to their kinship with salmon. Like all things, salmon is one of the Creator's children. All are interdependent inhabitants of Mother Earth, each here to make a contribution to the other so the Circle of Life can continue.

In Wet'suwet'en tradition, fishing can take on dangerous dimensions. There is no Tilley-hatted television host in a $40,000 boat with a high-powered motor and a sonar system pitching the adventure of spin-casting to armchair fishermen. This is the real thing, demanding great strength, dexterity, courage and nerves of steel.

The salmon harvest takes place from mid-June to mid-September. The various species include chinook, sockeye, coho and pink salmon and steelhead trout. The salmon, in their annual ritual of migration to their spawning grounds in quiet steams, courageously fight their way up the watersheds of the great Skeena and Fraser Rivers that etch their way through Wet'suwet'en territory. The banks are rough and rocky; in some places the rivers run through deep, steep canyons.

These are the fast, furious and unforgiving waters from which the

Wet'suwet'en harvest the salmon, armed with 32-foot gaff poles fitted with hooks, or the more modern dip-nets. As the salmon swim upriver, leaping up the fish ladders in the rapids, the men gaff or net them — many weighing as much as forty pounds — and run up the banks or canyon walls to deposit their catch. The feat is repeated until enough salmon are caught to feed everyone and provide for the winter.

Out of respect, the traditional Wet'suwet'en method of harvesting salmon guarantees that no more will be taken than is absolutely necessary. In the same vein, a clan will harvest only what they need from the waters or the land in their designated territory, and let the rest pass through. These practices ensure there will always be enough for others on this earth, and for future generations. There is a traditional saying attributed to Aboriginal peoples in the Pacific Northwest that speaks volumes about their belief systems and values: "We do not inherit the land from our ancestors, we borrow it from our grandchildren."

Some of the catch is eaten fresh. Most is dried, smoked or salted for the winter months, for feasts, gifts or payment. Nothing is wasted. Every part of the fish is used: the highly nutritious and delicious flesh and the calcium-rich bones are prepared in a great variety of tantalizing ways, many of which are to be found in the pages of *Feast!*

In the old days salmon and other products indigenous to the region were used as currency in trade between Wet'suwet'en and other nations of the Pacific Northwest. Trade items from the coastal peoples could include clams, eulachons, seaweed, halibut and *swinack,* a Native type of caviar. These goods would be exchanged for inland products — smoked or cured moose, venison and mountain goat and tanned hides. The trade routes were known as "grease trails" after the eulachon, a fish so rich in oil that when lit, it flames — the reason it is also known as the candlefish.

BANNOCK: THE NATIVE STAFF OF LIFE

If there is one food product common to virtually all Aboriginal peoples in Canada in one form or another, it is bannock, a bread for all seasons.

Originally it was an oatmeal or barley flatbread — *bannach* in Gaelic — brought over from Scotland by the fur traders, hunters, trappers and adventurers of the Hudson's Bay and North West Companies. They introduced it to Native peoples and it became a staple of company men and their Indian guides and wives on their onerous treks through the Canadian wilderness. Bannock was the ideal food for the trail. It had few ingredients, was very easy and quick to make, and was substantial and nourishing for the travel-weary and hungry at breakfast, midday and evening meals.

Over the past three hundred years it has been adopted as a Native staff of life by Aboriginal peoples from Truro to Tofino to Tuktoyaktuk, and all places in between. Many tales are told and even jokes are made about its preparation — on the trail, in the kitchen, out on the tundra, on the *sinaaq* ("ice floe edge" in Inuktitut, the language of the Inuit peoples). Its mouth-watering aroma will be sensed anywhere there's a fire, a skillet — or even a stick when an Aboriginal "pogo" is on the menu.

As will be seen in *Feast!*, bannock is a bread of incredible versatility, the only limitation on various styles for various occasions being the creativity of the baker. Only a few bannock recipes are included in these pages, but it could easily command an entire cookbook of its own.

No one knows bannock better or boasts more about who makes the best than Native hunters, trappers and prospectors. And Andrew George Sr., a hunter/trapper/prospector who has been making bannock in the bush for most of his seventy-ish years, tells the story of bannock this way:

> For generations we Wet'suwet'en trapped, hunted, fished and picked berries. We lived off the land and did not depend on any government. We were self-governing in our land in the true sense of the word. When we travelled the trails, all we packed were the necessities, especially flour, baking powder, salt and lard for bannock — and tea, of course.
>
> Here is how to make bannock over an open fire: First, for safety, build your fire by the water or areas where there is no grass. This is very important, for we must always protect our beautiful Mother Earth. Put the water on to boil for tea and make camp. Then mix the flour, salt, baking powder and water together in a tin bowl.
>
> Put some lard in the frying pan over the fire to melt and get it hot. Pat the bannock dough pieces into little thin cakes and place them in the pan to fry until they are golden brown. Another way is to put the whole dough in the pan and press it out at the edges so that it's about an inch and a half thick. Then sit it over the heat to brown the bottom a bit so it won't sag.

Then prop the pan up with a stick so the bannock is facing the fire and bake it, turning it every so often so that it cooks evenly.

These methods of cooking bannock are pretty universal among Native people across Canada and are even taught to white people whose jobs taken them out on the land — geologists, conservation officers, prospectors and the like.

I have to tell you a story about the white man and bannock in the early days.

Back then, Native people would see a white man out on the land getting ready to make his meal. If he didn't have a frying pan he would make up the bannock batter and throw it on the hot coals of a campfire. Then when he figured it was baked he would just take it off and blow the ashes from it. Why he didn't wrap it around a stick and cook it over the fire like some Native people do is beyond me. He must have been in an awful hurry for a feed of bannock and not care much about the charcoal around his mouth. Like I say, you can make bannock just about any way you want, but that one has to take the cake!

ANDREW GEORGE SR. (TSAIBESA)

WILD RICE: MAN-O-MIN

*I*n the Ojibwa language the word *man-o-min* derives from *Manitou* (the great Spirit) and *meenun* (delicacy). In English it is wild rice, but really it is a grain — the only wild cereal crop in Canada.

True wild rice is indigenous to northwestern Ontario, southwestern Manitoba and northern Minnesota, where it grows primarily in the shallows of lakes and rivers. It also grows in the cold lakes of Saskatchewan, the largest source of natural wild rice today.

Wild rice has been harvested by Native peoples in northwestern Ontario for more than 2,500 years. Traditionally, it held sacred status among the Ojibwa, and harvest time — late September to early October — was an occasion for families and friends to socialize, celebrate and give thanks to the Great Spirit for this wonderful gift. The early method of harvesting was to manoeuvre a canoe through the wild rice stands, and with sticks or paddles sweep the tall grass-like stalks inside the canoe so the grain would separate and drop to the bottom. Then the green rice was brought to shore, roasted to a shiny brownish black over an open fire, and placed in blankets or baskets and tossed in the air so the wind could blow away the husks.

Today the grain is cultivated in rice farms in some areas of the United States and Canada, but authentic wild rice is much larger, more flavourful and generally more nutritious than its commercial counterpart. True wild rice is one of Mother Earth's most perfect foods — high in fibre, low in fat, cholesterol-free and rich in minerals and the B vitamins. It has only 70 calories per half-cup serving. It also has a comforting chewy texture and a delicate nutty flavour. A bonus is that when cooked, a grain of natural wild rice expands as much as five times — a little goes a very long way.

Authentic wild rice, because of its flavour, nutritional value, versatility — and mystique — is earning a growing international reputation as the caviar of grains. It is featured in *Feast!* because it is one of Andrew's favourite accompaniments to many of his delicious creations.

*T*he recipes in *Feast!* are categorized under the components of our world — the waters, the earth, the land and the skies. Seafood and fish from the waters; fruits, vegetables and grains from the earth; deer, moose and rabbit from the land, and ducks, geese and ptarmigan from the skies. This is a neat and logical organization that will help the reader find recipes to experience.

But we had another reason for putting *Feast!* together in this manner. We wanted to pay our respects to Mother Earth and to each of the sources from which She offers Her bounties. For us it is a natural progression from the bottom up, so to speak. From the depths of the waters, through the earth, above to the land and up into the skies, where one day we will all face the Creator. If we have lived a life of honour and goodness toward each other, and we have respected all creatures and all things in our journey, we will meet with the Creator's approval.

So as you go through *Feast!*, don't just think of it as a book of wonderful, inspired recipes, but also enjoy the journey with us. As you walk in our moccasins, respect each recipe as a gift from Mother Earth and a blessing from the Creator.

It will add a new dimension to your reading and dining experience.

SO'H GA NEC KEWH DALHT! HAVE A GOOD MEAL!

BOOK TWO

THE SEASONS

Spirit Braid Seafood Platter, *page 46*

Feast! Seafood Spread

Baked Sweet Potato with Roasted
Hazelnuts, *page 80*

*F*or Aboriginal peoples, the seasons hold special significance. They signal transition, and each has its own special message for all creatures and all things within the waters and the earth, on the land and in the skies.

The yawning autumn, the sleep of winter, the awakening of spring and the dance of summer — the evening, the night, the morning and the afternoon of our eternity — are like signposts on our journey. So are infancy, adolescence, maturity and old age, the four directions and the four colours.

We respect the stages of our growth, the guideposts that point our way, the shadings that give us beauty and perspective, and the messengers of change that are the seasons. The Creator tells us we must be prepared to accept their blessings and sometimes their sorrows, for all are part of the Circle of Life.

In this section of *Feast!* we want to share some menus you can prepare that celebrate autumn, winter, spring and summer. Each recipe in the seasonal menus is found in its representative section in the book, either the Waters, the Earth, the Land or the Skies.

We invite you to prepare and enjoy them with your family and friends as the seasons come upon you. It is a nice way to create a special Aboriginal theme for a gathering centred around a season and to reflect upon the special significance it may hold for us.

Perhaps your guests could bring some small message of their own to explain what the season means to them as a way of adding to the celebration of your feast.

Autumn Feast Menus

The autumn is such a busy, lively time for the Wet'suwet'en. So much to do before the temperature drops and the snow flies. They go out on their territory, Now'h Yin'h Ta'h, to hunt moose, deer, elk, mountain goat and wild fowl.

For a time there is much fresh meat to share, but it must also be prepared for use during the long, cold winter months. And so it is smoked and dried in the old way, and frozen and canned in the modern way. It is the same with the huckleberries and blueberries and soapalillie, the root vegetables and the late corn. They too must be preserved for the winter so the people will have a balanced and healthy diet of meats and fruits and vegetables when fresh foods are in short supply.

There are few idle Wet'suwet'en hands in the autumn season, but it is also a good time to get together to enjoy the abundance of fresh food and the generosity of the Creator when the day's work is done.

Here are two of Andrew's favourite Autumn Feast menus typical of the season. Be sure to bring a good appetite with you when you prepare and enjoy these hearty creations.

MENU ONE

Wild Grouse Soup *(page 146)*

◆

Venison Steak Diane *(page 113)*

Fiddleheads Wabanaki *(page 75)*

Baked Sweet Potato with Roasted Hazelnuts *(page 80)*

Habe Sta (Wet'suwet'en Fry-Bread) *(page 87)*

◆

Stewed rhubarb

MENU TWO

Seafood Chowder Toody Ni *(page 41)*

◆

Braised Moose Ribs *(page 126)*

Roasted herb potatoes

Fried cabbage

Corn bread

◆

Poached crab apples

WINTER FEAST MENUS

*W*hen the pure white snow dresses Now'h Yin Ta'h in its finest winter coat with its evergreen fringes, the land takes on yet another beautiful hue.

It is supposed to be the slow season, and yet there is so much activity, so much to do. Of all the children of Mother Earth, only the bear sleeps the long sleep. The rest continue their quest for food and their struggle for survival.

Out on the territory Andrew Sr. and his sons pursue the fox, the marten and the lynx to contribute to their livelihood. They hunt the winter rabbit and grouse, and fish through the ice for trout and ling cod as welcome sources of fresh food. Of course there is much wood to be split, for fuel and cooking. The territory is such a cold place in winter.

But the homes of Tsaibesa and Gihl Lakh Khun are warm and comforting and friendly. Their kitchen wood stoves chatter their nonstop staccato crack and pop and hiss, morning, noon and night. Always on top of them is a pot of simmering soup and a kettle at the ready for tea. From their hot, dry ovens the ever-present smell of baking bannock tantalizes all who enter the room. Freshly laundered tea towels with the wonderful outdoor smell hang on racks at the side of the stove. They feel so warm to the touch when it is time to dry the dishes.

The large scrubbed wooden table in the centre of the room is an affable host, welcoming family and friends to sit together in its well-worn comfortable chairs, to talk, to tell stories, to laugh.

Wet'suwet'en kitchens are symphonies of sounds and sights, havens of lip-smacking tastes and inviting aromas that are especially heightened and pleasing in winter.

The dishes Andrew presents in these traditional Winter Feast menus are delicious and satisfying. Afterward, you may want to curl up before the fire and enjoy another Canadian winter tradition — "Hockey Night in Canada."

MENU ONE

Wild Rabbit Soup *(page 132)*

◆

Half-Dried Salmon *(page 49)*

Parsley Potatoes *(page 81)*

Boiled mixed greens (turnip, beet tops)

Deep-Fried Bannock *(page 88)*

◆

Huckleberry and apple crumble

MENU TWO

Wild Duck and Winter Vegetable Soup *(page 147)*

◆

Aboriginal Mixed Grill *(page 129)*

Boiled cabbage and root vegetables

Wild Rice and Mushrooms *(page 77)*

Fresh baked yeast rolls

◆

Fresh squeezed huckleberries

SPRING FEAST MENUS

The fireweed is first to peek through the melting snow and herald the arriving season. It is time to stretch, yawn one last time, and waken to the fresh, noisy spring.

The honking of the endless flights of Canada geese coming home from their winter vacations, the stirring of the animals in the bush, the roar of the rivers made more furious by the spring runoff, the ear-splitting crack of spring ice.

In Now'h Yin'h Ta'h the long winter has finally passed, and thanks are given for all that it has offered the Wet'suwet'en. Life can now begin another cycle. The spring rains quench the thirst of the trees and plants and wildflowers. As their boughs, branches and stems sway gently in the drying wind, they sprout their foliage and the tapestry of the season becomes vibrantly colourful once again.

This is a good time to catch the spring whitefish and trout, to hunt the blue grouse and beaver. Soon it will be time to harvest the wild spring vegetables and herbs — celery, garlic and onions. And how the children love the sweet sap of the jack pine!

Andrew's Spring Feast menus reflect the spirit and flavour of Wet'suwet'en life during this wonderful time of year.

Menu One

Boiled Herring Roe on Kelp (*page 62*)

◆

Stuffed Moose Heart with Gravy (*page 128*)

Oven roasted potatoes

Mixture of root vegetables

Tsaibesa's Bannock (*page 84*)

◆

Saskatoon pie

Menu Two

Steamed Clams with Eulachon Butter (*page 64*)

◆

Baked Halibut on Rice with Seaweed (*page 56*)

Dilled carrots

Fresh whole wheat rolls

◆

Cold wild cranberry soup

SUMMER FEAST MENUS

*I*n the valleys and meadows the warm summer sun bathes and nourishes every berry and blade of grass, the gentle summer rain cleanses and refreshes all creatures and things in Wet'suwet'en territory.

First there are the rich, red wild strawberries. After a time there are the deep purple saskatoons, and the delightful sweet-tart raspberries and blackberries to fill the baskets of the pickers to overflowing. In late summer the huckleberry, blueberry and wild cranberry bushes present their juicy offerings, to eat fresh and to can for later on.

In summer, along canyons and rocky banks of the rivers of Kya'h wiget and Hagwilget, strong, fearless Wet'suwet'en with long gaff poles and nets scoop large fish from the fast, foamy waters. With luck there will be sockeye and chinook and coho and steelhead. The salmon harvest is in full swing in Now'h Yin'h Ta'h. Some of the catch will be eaten fresh and the rest will be dried or smoked or canned for another time. The drying racks and smoke houses are full and the aroma of salmon permeates the territory.

It is the best time to cook outdoors, over a campfire or a barbecue. So many of Andrew's recipes in *Feast!* can be cooked this way, and his Summer Feast menus are no exception.

Menu One

Venison Consommé *(page 104)*

◆

Pacific Salmon and Atlantic Fiddlehead Stir-Fry *(page 45)*

Fresh baked rolls

Corn bread

◆

Taas Guz (Cold Huckleberry Soup) *(page 94)*

Menu Two

Barbecued Oysters *(page 67)*

◆

Rabbit Stew *(page 133)*

Fresh crusty rolls

◆

Upsidedown blueberry cake

BOOK THREE

RECIPES

FROM
THE
WATERS

The creatures from the waters — the ocean, the lakes, the rivers and streams — have been instrumental in shaping the lives of Aboriginal peoples of the Pacific Northwest. From the beginning these foods have been available to them in great abundance, permitting a less-nomadic existence than, say, that of the Cree, Blackfoot and Métis Nations, whose survival depended on the buffalo herds that roamed freely over the vast Canadian prairies and respected no borders. It was a way of life that gave rise to the tipi, a light, portable and quickly assembled "house" that accommodated their families as they pursued their sustenance.

The coastal peoples, on the other hand, were able to set up permanent communities and build permanent homes, called long houses. These were fairly large buildings made from cedar logs, with cedar shingle roofs. Each long house would accommodate a clan, with as many as five families.

In summer the Wet'suwet'en would travel downriver to Hagwilget and Kya'h wiget to harvest the salmon and preserve it for the winter months. In the old days it took Andrew's grandparents Gisdewe, Tsaibesa and their families at least five days by horse and wagon to make their way from Beewini Bin (Owen Lake) to Hagwilget to get their salmon.

The recipes in "From the Waters" are only a sample of some of the foods enjoyed by the peoples of the Pacific Northwest.

Salmon Soup Wet'suwet'en

This is a traditional soup of the Aboriginal peoples of the Pacific Northwest. As with so many traditional recipes I have added a few contemporary twists. After all, one of the reasons Aboriginal peoples have survived for thousands of years is that we have been able to adapt to changing times while maintaining our traditional values. The same holds true for our foods.

You will notice I insist on Pacific salmon in this recipe. My Olympic team mate and friend Bryan Sappier may think differently but that is only because he doesn't know what real salmon tastes like. (He is from the Malecite Nation in New Brunswick).

Sorry Bryan, friends are friends, but when it comes to salmon . . . ! Actually, you can use the other stuff . . . if you really have to.

4 cups (1 L) fish stock or water

¼ lb. (125 g) salmon roe

1 lb. (500 g) fresh Pacific salmon, cubed

½ lb. (250 g) potato, diced

1 stalk celery, diced

1 medium onion, diced

Sea salt and pepper to taste

Pinch curry powder

1 bay leaf

Dry seaweed (p. 68) for garnish

- In a large soup pot, bring stock to a simmer.
- Heat salmon roe in a small saucepan and add to soup stock.
- Add salmon, potato, celery, onion, salt, pepper, curry powder and bay leaf.
- Bring to boil. Simmer over low heat until potatoes are just tender. Discard bay leaf.
- Ladle into soup bowls and sprinkle with dry seaweed.

Serve with hot bannock.

SERVES 4.

SEAFOOD CHOWDER TOODY NI

This rich and delicious chowder was a favourite with customers at my Toody Ni Grill. It can be a meal in itself with bannock, though it is also great as a soup course in a full dinner — provided you don't get too carried away with the serving size. Serve a small bowl or cupful as one course in a wonderful Native feast for all your guests.

You can find seaweed at many fish markets and some specialty stores.

8 cups (2 L) fish stock or water

½ cup (125 mL) bacon fat or butter

1 medium onion, diced

1 stalk celery, diced

4 cloves garlic, crushed

1 bay leaf

½ cup (125 mL) all-purpose flour

¼ lb. (125 g) potato, diced

1 medium carrot, diced

½ green pepper, diced

⅓ lb. (175 g) fresh clams

⅓ lb. (175 g) salmon, cubed

⅓ lb. (175 g) red snapper, cubed

Salt and pepper to taste

½ cup (125 mL) (approx.) whipping cream

- In a large saucepan, bring fish stock to a boil.

- In a large heavy soup pot over medium-high heat, heat bacon fat. Sauté onion, celery, garlic and bay leaf until onions are transparent.

- Stir in flour and cook, stirring, 2 minutes. (The result is what chefs call a roux.) Slowly add hot stock to the roux, stirring well to prevent lumps. Bring to a simmer.

- Add potato, carrot and green pepper; simmer until vegetables are tender.

- Add clams, salmon and red snapper. Cook over low heat until fish is cooked through and tender, about 10 minutes. Discard bay leaf. Season with salt and pepper.

- Remove from heat and stir in just enough cream to turn the chowder white.

SERVES 10 TO 12 AS A STARTER, 6 TO 8 AS A MAIN COURSE.

FISH STOCK

Fish stock has many uses — in soups, chowders, sauces and for making the Court Bouillon (p. 43) for poaching fish. Here are two ways I prepare fish stock. The first is a little bit simpler, but both produce great results.

Remember: always use cold *water in any stock you make.*

> 4 lb. (2 kg) bones of whitefish, halibut, sole, turbot, etc.
>
> 5 qt. (5 L) cold water
>
> 2 medium onions, thinly sliced
>
> ½ cup (125 mL) chopped mushrooms
>
> ½ bunch parsley stalks
>
> 1 bay leaf
>
> 12 peppercorns, crushed
>
> 1 tsp. (5 mL) fennel seeds
>
> Juice of 1 lemon

METHOD #1

- Wash fish bones and place in a large heavy soup pot. Add water and bring to a boil. Skim foam off the surface of the stock.

- Add onions, mushrooms, parsley stalks, bay leaf, peppercorns, fennel seeds and lemon juice. Simmer, uncovered, for 30 to 45 minutes, skimming surface occasionally.

- Strain stock through a fine sieve.

- Stock will keep for at least a week in the fridge. Or you can boil the strained stock until it starts to thicken, about 3 to 4 hours. Pour into a large baking or roasting pan and chill a few hours until set. Cut gel into cubes, wrap in plastic wrap and freeze. Whenever you need fresh stock, take a cube from the freezer and dilute with hot water. (You can freeze any stock this way.)

METHOD #2

- In a large, heavy soup pot, sauté onions, parsley flakes, bay leaf, peppercorns and fennel seeds in 1 tbsp. (10 mL) butter until onion is transparent.

- Add a squirt of fresh lemon juice, fish bones and mushrooms. Add water and bring to a simmer; simmer, uncovered, for 30 to 45 minutes, skimming the surface occasionally.

- Strain, cool and store as above.

MAKES 5 QT. (5 L).

Court Bouillon for Poaching Fish

A much more flavourful and professional way of poaching fish than simply using water.

½ large carrot, thinly sliced

½ large onion, thinly sliced

1 stalk celery, thinly sliced

6 black peppercorns, crushed

5 parsley stalks

1 bay leaf

1 tbsp. (15 mL) salt

¾ cup (175 mL) white wine vinegar

8 cups (2 L) cold fish stock or water

- In a large heavy soup pot, place carrot, onion, celery, peppercorns, parsley stalks, bay leaf, salt, vinegar and fish stock. Bring to a boil, reduce heat and simmer, uncovered, for 20 minutes.

- Add the fresh fish to be poached and simmer until fish is tender, allowing 5 to 8 minutes per pound (500 g).

MAKES 8 CUPS (2 L).

BROILED SALMON

After a long day at work, this is a very quick and simple way to enjoy a meal. Serve with rice or potatoes and your favourite vegetable.

4 6-oz. (175-g) salmon fillets

2 tsp. (10 mL) vegetable oil

1 tsp. (5 mL) lemon juice

Salt and pepper to taste

- Preheat broiler about 10 minutes.
- Rub both sides of salmon with oil, lemon juice, salt and pepper.
- Broil 7 to 8 minutes each side.

SERVES 4.

PACIFIC SALMON AND ATLANTIC FIDDLEHEAD STIR-FRY

In this dish, east meets west twice, if you get my meaning. It is fantastic!

1 2-lb (1-kg) fresh Pacific salmon,
skin and bones removed

3 cloves garlic, minced

1 tsp. (5 mL) minced gingerroot

Salt and pepper to taste

2 tbsp. (25 mL) vegetable oil

1½ lb. (750 g) fresh or frozen fiddleheads

2 tbsp. (25 mL) white wine

½ cup (125 mL) teriyaki sauce

1 tsp. (5 mL) cornstarch

- Cut salmon into bite-sized pieces. Toss with garlic, ginger, salt and pepper.

- Over high heat, heat oil in a wok or large skillet to smoking point. Add salmon; stir-fry until lightly browned. Add fiddleheads; stir-fry for another minute or two.

- Add wine and cook, stirring frequently, until wine is reduced by half. Stir in teriyaki sauce.

- In a small bowl, blend cornstarch with 3 tbsp. (50 mL) water; add to wok and stir until thickened.

Serve over a bed of wild rice or steamed rice.

SERVES 4.

SPIRIT BRAID SEAFOOD PLATTER
WITH SAMBUCA FIDDLEHEAD SAUCE

It is said that when the hair is woven together, the Spirit is in the braids. By weaving the red salmon and the white halibut together, the spirit of friendship between us is symbolized. When you serve this dish to your family and friends, tell them what it means. It will add to the enjoyment of an outstanding meal that is fairly exotic but easy to make.

> 2 4-oz. (125 g) strips Pacific salmon
>
> 1 4-oz. (125-g) strip halibut or cod
>
> 2 cups (500 mL) Court Bouillon (p. 43)
>
> Sambuca Fiddlehead Sauce (recipe follows)

- Braid three strips of fish (two salmon and one white fish) like you would hair. Skewer both ends with toothpicks to hold braid together.

- In a large skillet, bring Court Bouillon to a simmer. Place braids carefully in a pan and poach 12 to 14 minutes, until fish is tender.

- Remove fish from liquid and drain on paper towels.

- Arrange wild rice (p. 77) on one side of a platter. Drizzle some Sambuca Fiddlehead Sauce beside it, gently place over the braided fish on top and drizzle a little more sauce over it.

SERVES 4.

SAMBUCA FIDDLEHEAD SAUCE

> 1 tbsp. (15 mL) unsalted butter
>
> 3 shallots, finely chopped
>
> 1 clove garlic, finely chopped
>
> 2 tbsp. (25 mL) Sambuca
>
> 1 cup (250 mL) whipping cream
>
> 2 oz. (50 g) fiddleheads, parboiled and drained

- In a medium skillet over medium-high heat, melt butter. Sauté shallots and garlic until shallots are softened.

- Carefully stir in Sambuca; reduce by half.

- Stir in cream and simmer until sauce thickens slightly. Add fiddleheads and simmer, stirring until fiddleheads are heated through.

MAKES ABOUT 1 CUP (250 ML).

SALT SALMON

Don't be alarmed by what seems to be a lot of salt in this recipe. It is drawn out through the overnight soaking, leaving the salmon very tender and moist.

> **1 side filleted coho or sockeye salmon**
> **(about 5 lb./2.2 kg), skin on,**
> **head and tail removed**
>
> **2 cups (500 mL) rock salt**

- In a large nonreactive baking dish, spread half the rock salt. Lay salmon over salt and top with remaining salt. Refrigerate, covered, overnight.

- Remove salmon from salt and soak overnight in water to draw out salt, changing water several times.

- In a large pot, bring water to a boil. Pat salmon dry, remove skin and cut salmon into six 8-oz (250-g) pieces.

- Boil salmon pieces 10 to 14 minutes or until fish flakes easily.

Serve with steamed rice topped with chopped dry seaweed and Sautéed Wild Celery (p. 76).

SERVES 4 TO 6.

SMOKED SALMON WET'SUWET'EN STYLE

We call smoked salmon Be'h. Most people don't have their own smoke houses, but the compact smoker unit that can be purchased for home use at a reasonable price is an acceptable alternative. It can also be used for meats, cheeses and many other products, so it is a good appliance to have.

1 whole sockeye or coho salmon, 7 to 10 lb. (3.5 to 4.5 kg), head and tail on

Salt and pepper

- Prepare smoke house or smoker unit using cold smoke (no fire, just smoke).

- Season salmon inside and out with salt and pepper. Hang salmon in smoke house for 1 to 1½ days, until skin gets hard.

- Working from inside the fish and being careful not to cut through the skin, cut along both sides of the backbone from the head end to the tail; remove backbone and tail. Open up fish and lay flat.

- Cut thin lengthwise strips off salmon. Return to smoke house for 1½ days for half-dried, 2½ to 3 days for *Be'h*, or full-dried.

8 TO 10 PEOPLE CAN BE SERVED FROM ONE SALMON.

HALF-DRIED SALMON

Yet another way to prepare this tasty delicacy.

4 8-oz. (250-g) portions half-dried salmon

8 cups (2 L) Court Bouillon (p. 43) or cold water

1 tsp. (5 mL) salt

- Put salmon in a large saucepan and add Court Bouillon and salt.

- Bring to a boil; reduce heat and simmer 8 to 10 minutes.

- Serve with drawn butter (p. 69) and Parsley Potatoes (p. 81), with fiddleheads or Sautéed Wild Celery (p. 76).

SERVES 4.

SMOKED SALMON LINGUINE

Here's a combination of cultures and tastes to delight the palate.

½ lb. (250 g) linguine

¼ cup (50 mL) cream cheese

2 tbsp. (25 mL) white wine

2 sprigs fresh dill, chopped
(or 1 tsp./5 mL dried dillweed)

2 cloves garlic, minced

2 cups (500 mL) whipping cream

1½ lb. (750 g) smoked salmon, thinly sliced

¼ cup (50 mL) freshly grated Parmesan cheese

Salt and pepper to taste

4 green onions, thinly sliced

* In a large pot of boiling salted water, cook linguine until tender but firm. Drain and return to pot. Meanwhile, in a medium saucepan, combine cream cheese, wine, dill and garlic; simmer until reduced by half. Stir in cream, smoked salmon and Parmesan; return to a simmer.

* Add drained linguine, and toss well. Simmer until sauce starts to thicken slightly. Season with salt and pepper.

Serve topped with chopped green onion and additional Parmesan.

SERVES 4.

SMOKED SALMON ON BANNOCK FINGERS

A terrific appetizer with a Native touch. To save time, you can bake the bannock the day before.

1 whole baked bannock (p. 84), cooled

1 lb. (500 g) smoked salmon chunks

¼ cup (50 mL) cream cheese

½ tsp. (2 mL) lemon juice

Dash Worcestershire sauce

Salt and pepper to taste

Lemon slices and fresh parsley, for garnish

- Cut bannock into ¼-inch (5-mm slices).

- In a food processor, blend salmon, cream cheese, lemon juice, Worcestershire, salt and pepper until smooth.

- Using a piping bag, pipe onto bannock slices. Cut each slice into ¼-inch-wide (5-mm) "fingers."

- Arrange on a platter and garnish with lemon slices and parsley.

MAKES APPROXIMATELY 50 HORS D'OEUVRES.

Campfire BBQ Salmon Wet'suwet'en Style

(Woven with Willow Branches on an Alder Stick)

The Wet'suwet'en use alder in the barbecue pit and smoke house because it gives off good heat and flavour. Pine, poplar and cedar contain sap that gives off black smoke, turning your salmon black and giving it an unusual taste.

> 1 whole salmon, 7 to 10 lb. (3.5 to 4.5 kg), head and tail on
>
> Salt and pepper to taste
>
> 1 alder stick, ¼ in. (5 mm) thick and 3 to 4 ft. (1 to 1.2 m) long, bark removed
>
> 4 willow sticks, 18 in. (45 cm) long

- Prepare smoke house or smoker unit using hot smoke (with fire). Hang salmon in smoker at least 3 to 4 hours or overnight, until skin is firm.

- Build a large campfire and let burn down to hot coals.

- Using a very sharp knife, remove head and cut around gills, removing all bones. Working from inside the fish and being careful not to cut through the skin, cut along both sides of the backbone from the head end to the tail; remove backbone and tail. Open up fish and lay flat.

- Weave the alder stick through the fish where the backbone was. Weave willow sticks from side to side through the fish to keep it open and flat. Season with salt and pepper.

- Stab salmon stick into the ground about 1 ft. (30 cm) from the coals, skin side facing the fire, and cook for 20 minutes. Turn salmon around and cook for another 20 to 25 minutes.

Serve with baked potatoes cooked right in the hot coals, boiled sweet corn and warm bannock.

SERVES 10 TO 12.

PAN-FRIED STURGEON

Most people know that caviar is the roe of sturgeon. But the fish itself has a firm flesh and a slightly strong flavour, somewhere between mackerel and whitefish. In the old days the Wet'suwet'en would trade for sturgeon with Native peoples from the Fraser River and the coast.

1 6-oz. (175-g) sturgeon fillet

Salt and pepper to taste

Splash lemon juice

Splash Worcestershire sauce

2 tbsp. (25 mL) unsalted butter

- Lay sturgeon in a glass baking dish and season with salt, pepper, lemon juice and Worcestershire sauce. Marinate, covered, for 30 minutes.

- In a large skillet over medium-high heat, brown the butter, being careful not to burn it. Fry sturgeon 2 to 3 minutes each side. Transfer to plate and pour butter from skillet over sturgeon.

To give this dish a Native twist, serve with steamed rice topped with chopped dry seaweed and fresh steamed vegetables.

SERVES 1.

Pan-fried Trout

This is a favourite spring dish — fresh fish after a long winter of dried salmon.

1 whole trout, 1½ to 2 lb. (750 g to 1 kg)

1 cup (250 mL) all-purpose flour

Salt and pepper to taste

3 tbsp. (50 mL) bacon fat or vegetable oil

- In a shallow dish, combine flour, salt and pepper.

- In a large cast-iron skillet over medium-high heat, melt bacon fat. Dredge trout in seasoned flour; brown on both sides.

- Transfer trout to a baking sheet and cook in 375°F (190°C) oven 5 to 7 minutes, until fish flakes easily.

Serve with mashed potatoes and fresh vegetables.

Serves 1.

Trout Almondine with a Native Touch

Trout have abounded in Wet'suwet'en territory for thousands of years. The "almondine" thing is a contemporary addition, and I'm glad it came along.

1 tbsp. (15 mL) slivered almonds

½ cup (125 mL) all-purpose flour

Salt and pepper to taste

2 tbsp. (25 mL) unsalted butter

1 8-oz. (250 g) brook or speckled trout, boned if desired

- In a large skillet over medium-high heat, toast the almonds, stirring frequently, until golden brown. Transfer almonds to a small bowl.

- In a shallow dish, combine flour, salt and pepper.

- In the skiller, melt butter over medium-high heat. Dredge trout in seasoned flour and cook 7 to 9 minutes each side, until lightly browned. Transfer trout to a serving plate, sprinkle with almonds and pour over pan juices.

For the Native touch, serve with Wild Rice and Mushrooms (p. 77) and Fiddleheads Wabanaki (p. 75).

SERVES 1.

Baked Halibut on Rice with Seaweed

Halibut is a universal favourite, and the addition of rice and seaweed makes it that much better.

4 6-oz. (175-g) halibut fillets

Salt and pepper to taste

- Place fillet in a shallow baking dish. Sprinkle with salt and pepper.
- Cover with buttered foil or parchment paper.
- Bake at 400°F (200°C) for 12 minutes or until fish flakes easily.
- Arrange fish on a serving platter with a border of wild rice or steamed white rice topped with chopped dry seaweed.

Serve with bannock.

SERVES 4.

Salmon Soup Wetsu'wet'en, *page 40*

Pacific Salmon and Atlantic Fiddlehead
Stir-Fry, *page 45*

Seafood Chowder Toody Ni, *page 41*

Smoked Salmon on Bannock Fingers,
page 51

Fried Halibut

This reminds me of a corny sign in a fish-and-chip shop: "We fry fish for the halibut." Sorry!

¼ cup (50 mL) all-purpose flour

Salt and pepper to taste

2 tbsp. (25 mL) vegetable oil

4 6-oz. (175-g) halibut steaks

2 tbsp. (25 mL) unsalted butter

1 large onion, thinly sliced

Juice of 1 lemon

- In a shallow dish, combine flour, salt and pepper.
- In a cast-iron skillet over medium-high heat, heat oil to the smoking point.
- Dredge halibut steaks in seasoned flour and fry 7 to 8 minutes each side, until fish flakes easily.
- Transfer steaks to a heated platter and keep warm.
- In the same pan, melt butter; sauté onion with salt, pepper and lemon juice until onion is transparent.

Top steaks with onions and serve with rice topped with chopped dry seaweed.

Serves 4.

BOILED SALMON ROE WITH SEAWEED

You may think roe — fish eggs — is an acquired taste, but once you try it you will find it is a delicious beginning to a Native meal. Eulachon butter — also called eulachon grease — is made from the fish, which belongs to the smelt family. The fish were fermented in tubs, and the strained oil was stored. It is very rich in flavour and high in nutrients and vitamins. However, it is difficult to find, so you can substitute drawn or clarified butter, which goes well with most seafood.

> 2 lb. (1 kg) spring salmon roe
>
> 1 tsp. (5 mL) salt
>
> 2 tsp. (10 mL) chopped dry seaweed (p. 68)
>
> 1 tsp. eulachon butter or drawn butter (p. 69)

◆ In a large saucepan, bring roe, salt and 6 cups (1.5 L) water to a boil; reduce heat and simmer, uncovered, 20 to 30 minutes, or until roe hardens and turns a pale orange. Drain roe and return to pot. Stir in seaweed and drawn or eulachon butter.

Serve in bowls with steamed rice.

SERVES 4.

Boiled Smoked Eulachons

The smoking gives this delicious little fish an intriguing flavour.

24 smoked eulachons

- Cut eulachons in half along the backbone.
- Place in a large saucepan with enough water to cover. Bring to a boil, reduce heat and simmer 5 minutes.

Serve with chopped dry seaweed and rice.

Serves 4.

DRIED OR SMOKED EULACHONS

Once again, smelts will work as a substitute.

5 to 500 small fish

- To dry eulachons, hang them on open-air racks for 2 to 4 days.

- To smoke eulachons, hang them in your smoker in a cold smoke for 2 to 4 days, depending on their size and how dry you want them to be. (This is the same procedure the Wet'suwet'en use to smoke salmon, only we use large smoke houses.)

MAKES ENOUGH FOR A SMALL OR VERY LARGE GATHERING OF WET'SUWET'EN!

Pan-fried Eulachons or Smelts

Simple to prepare, but oh, so delicious!

2 cups (500 mL) all-purpose flour

Salt and pepper to taste

2 to 3 tbsp. (25 to 50 mL) lard or vegetable oil

24 eulachons or smelts

- In a shallow dish, combine flour, salt and pepper.

- In a cast-iron skillet over high heat, heat lard to the smoking point, then reduce heat to medium. Dredge eulachons in seasoned flour and fry 5 to 7 minutes each side, until golden brown.

Serve with chopped dry seaweed and wild rice or steamed white rice.

SERVES 4.

BOILED HERRING ROE ON KELP

Coastal Native people harvested herring roe in two ways, one by submerging nets on racks with kelp (a form of seaweed) hanging from them, and leaving them on underwater racks until the herring spawned on the kelp. The other was by felling trees along the inlets into the water, so the herring would spawn on the branches. Then the people would wade into the inlet and remove the branches covered with the herring roe.

It was worth the effort, because herring roe has a nice caviar taste and the kelp a crispy consistency.

2 lb. (1 kg) herring roe on kelp

½ cup (125 mL) eulachon butter or drawn butter

- Soak herring roe in cold water overnight to extract salt (herring roe is preserved in coarse salt).

- Rinse and drain roe and cut into bite-sized peices.

- Bring a large pot of water to the boil and boil herring pieces 4 to 5 minutes, until roe turns bright white. Drain well.

- Return roe to pan, cover with water, and boil another 4 to 5 minutes. (This second boiling is not necessary if you are using fresh roe.)

Serve hot or at room temperature with eulachon butter or drawn butter for dipping.

SERVES 4.

Pan-fried Herring Roe on Kelp

Either way of preparing the dish, boiling or pan-frying, makes for a nice snack at home in the evening, or as a treat for guests.

2 lb. (1 kg) herring roe on kelp

2 tbsp. (25 mL) unsalted butter

½ cup (125 mL) eulachon butter or drawn butter

- Soak herring roe in cold water overnight to extract salt.

- Rinse and drain roe and cut into bite-sized pieces.

- In a large skillet over medium-high heat, melt butter. Sauté roe pieces until roe turns bright white.

Serve with eulachon butter or drawn butter for dipping.

SERVES 4 TO 6.

STEAMED PACIFIC NORTHWEST CLAMS WITH EULACHON BUTTER

I believe this standby for seafood lovers is enhanced by the eulachon butter, as are all recipes where it is included. It is what gives them a unique flavour. I just wish it was more widely available so more people could find out for themselves.

> 50 butter clams
>
> 1 cup (250 mL) fish stock or water
>
> ⅓ cup (75 mL) chopped dry seaweed (p. 68)
>
> 2 tsp. (10 mL) eulachon butter

- Rinse clams thoroughly to remove sand and discard any opened clams.

- Set a large saucepan or skillet over medium-high heat for 5 minutes. Add clams, fish stock, seaweed and eulachon butter. Cover and shake pan vigorously.

- Steam clams 8 to 10 minutes, until they open. Discard any clams that do not open.

- Pour clams with their juices onto a serving platter or bowl.

Serve with bannock or sourdough bread, another Pacific Northwest favourite, or pour over a bowl of steamed rice.

SERVES 2.

Pan-fried Clams with Seaweed

*A*nother wonderful way to enjoy clams.

> 2 lb. (1 kg) butter clams, steamed and shelled, juices reserved
>
> 1 tbsp. (15 mL) eulachon butter or drawn butter
>
> 2 shallots, finely diced
>
> 1 clove garlic, minced
>
> 2 tsp. (10 mL) chopped dry seaweed (p. 68)
>
> 2 tsp. (10 mL) fish stock or cold water
>
> Salt and pepper to taste

- Chop clams; set aside.
- In a large skillet over medium heat, heat eulachon grease. Sauté shallots and garlic until shallots are transparent. Add clams and sauté 2 more minutes. Add seaweed, fish stock and reserved juices from clams. Simmer just until heated through.
- Season to taste with salt and pepper.

Serve on a bed of steamed rice.

SERVES 4.

CLAM FRITTERS

These fritters make a tasty snack, especially when dipped in spicy dill sauce.

1 cup (250 mL) baby clams, shelled, chopped

1 medium onion, chopped

1 stalk celery, chopped

3 cups (750 mL) all-purpose flour

2 eggs

4 tsp. (20 mL) baking powder

¼ cup (50 mL) water

- Mix clams, onion and celery.
- In another bowl, mix flour, eggs, baking powder and water.
- Add clam mixture to the batter. Mix.
- Let batter sit for 1 hour.
- Using 2 tablespoons, drop batter into hot deep fryer.
- Cook until golden brown.

Serve with dill sauce, for dipping, and crisp salad.

SERVES 6 TO 8.

BARBECUED OYSTERS

Cross-hatching the oysters has nothing to do with breeding; it's a style of cooking.

1 tbsp. (15 mL) vegetable oil

1 tsp. (5 mL) lemon juice

Salt and pepper to taste

24 freshly shucked oysters

- Prepare barbecue, or preheat broiler.
- In a small bowl, mix oil, lemon juice, salt and pepper. Brush mixture over oysters.
- Place oysters on the grill on a diagonal and cook 2 minutes.
- Turn oysters in the other direction to get cross-hatched grill marks; cook another 2 minutes.
- Flip oysters over and repeat the process on the other side. (Alternatively, broil oysters about 4 inches from the heat, 2 to 3 minutes each side, turning once.)

Serve with drawn butter for dipping.

SERVES 4.

Dry Seaweed

Many of my dishes call for dry seaweed, because it complements seafood so well. In the old days my people used it as a seasoning, since it has such a high salt content. It's especially tasty when added to rice or soup. I've loved it since I was a child and you will too. But don't eat too much — I want you to save room for the rest of your meal. Here's how we do it.

We gather the seaweed from the ocean and hang it on open-air racks to dry for 2 or 3 days. Or we dry the seaweed for a day and then hang it in a smoke house or a smoker for another day. Lightly smoked, it takes on a unique flavour.

Japanese seaweed can be used. It can be found in some speciality stores and health food stores.

DRAWN BUTTER FOR SEAFOOD

What hat would seafood recipes be without drawn butter!

2 lb. (1 kg) unsalted butter

- In a saucepan over low heat, melt butter.
- When butter comes to a slow boil, skim the surface.
- Continue cooking and skimming until the butter is clear, making sure the butter does not burn.
- Remove from heat and let stand a few minutes. Carefully pour the clear yellow liquid into a bowl, leaving the white milk solids in the pan.

Will keep, refrigerated, for two weeks.

MAKES 8 TO 10 OZ. (250 TO 300 ML).

FROM
THE
EARTH

*I*t is Mother Earth who gives us the place from which the grass and trees and flowers grow, from which the fireweed emerges in spring. Her love and warmth nurture the young seedlings, sprouts and shoots that grow and mature into the fruits and berries, vegetables and grains that are brothers and sisters to the creatures from the waters, the land and the skies.

The Wet'suwet'en have always harvested the offerings from Mother Earth, the wild fruits and vegetables that grow abundantly throughout their territories. Along with fish, wild meat and fowl, they have been important sources of nutrition and have provided interesting variety and diverse flavours to the Wet'suwet'en diet.

Gathering these gifts from Mother Earth was a family activity for Andrew, his mother and father, brothers and sisters, where all shared in the work of the harvest and the joyful time of togetherness.

This section of *Feast!* features recipes that Andrew has created from some of the gifts of Mother Earth — from the soapalillie berry indigenous to Now'h Yin'h Ta'h, to the fiddlehead fern that springs from the ground thousands of miles to the east. It offers a wonderful cross-section of tempting dishes to accompany main courses, to savour on their own, or to provide memorable sweet and tasty conclusions to the Native dining experience. Most are fairly simple yet hearty dishes, with an added Aboriginal flair.

WILD FLOWER SALAD

Long, long before yuppie nouvelle-cuisine chefs were even thought of, my people were making salads with wild ingredients. Here is a modern-day version of a recipe that is as old as the hills. It is a terrific way to begin an adventure in Aboriginal dining.

½ cup (125 mL) watercress

1 cup (250 mL) dandelion greens

½ cup (125 mL) Belgian endive leaves (about 2 endives)

½ cup (125 mL) rose petals

1 cup (250 mL) baby lettuce leaves

Other seasonal edible flowers such as buttercups, violets, wild roses

½ cup (125 mL) chopped fresh herbs to taste

- Wash all flowers gently in ice-cold water to clean and refresh them.

- Drain thoroughly and pat dry on paper towels. Wash, drain and spin dry the greens. Toss flowers and greens together in a large salad bowl with herbs, a light splash of simple vinaigrette and freshly ground pepper.

SERVES 6 TO 8.

FIDDLEHEADS WABANAKI

*M*ore and more people are coming to know the delights of a great wild vegetable known as the fiddlehead. The very best of these shoots from a young fern plant come from New Brunswick. The Micmac, Maliseet, Abenaki, Passamaquoddy and Penobscot nations of the Maritimes and Maine have harvested this culinary delight for centuries. I have named this recipe in honour of them.

This is an updated version of what their great-grandmothers prepared. I love it because of its incredible versatility. It goes so well with virtually any Aboriginal dish, and that is why you find it suggested so often in Feast!

½ lb (250 g) fresh or frozen fiddleheads

1 slice bacon, cut into ½-inch (1-cm) pieces

1 tbsp. (15 mL) unsalted butter

1 large shallot, sliced

2 cloves garlic, crushed

Pinch each sea salt and pepper

- Wash fresh fiddleheads thoroughly to remove dirt. In a large pot of boiling salted water, blanch fiddleheads 3 minutes. Drain in a colander, refresh under cold water, and drain well again. Set aside.

- In a large skillet over medium heat, cook bacon, stirring occasionally, until crisp; remove bacon with a slotted spoon and drain on paper towels. Chop.

- Pour off all but 2 tsp. (10 mL) fat. Increase heat to medium-high and in the fat melt the butter. Sauté shallots and garlic until shallots are transparent and soft.

- Add fiddleheads and sauté 5 minutes. Remove from heat and season with salt and pepper.

Serve topped with bacon bits.

SERVES 2.

Sautéed Coos (Wild Celery)

Coos is one vegetable indigenous to my part of the world. If you use true wild celery, you can make this dish only in the first two weeks of June. The rest of the year you can use regular celery, but the taste isn't quite the same.

¼ lb. (125 g) wild celery

2 slices bacon, cut into ½-inch (1-cm) pieces

Salt and pepper to taste

- Peel the bitter outer skin off the wild celery and cut celery into ½-inch (1-cm) pieces.

- In a cast-iron skillet over medium-high heat, cook bacon, stirring occasionally, until crisp. Add celery; sauté, stirring, 3 to 4 minutes or until tender-crisp.

Season with salt and pepper and serve immediately.

Serves 4.

WILD RICE AND MUSHROOMS

Wild rice has a flavour that is complemented very well by mushrooms. It is becoming favoured all over the world, and I am proud to say that it is one of Canada's indigenous products, just like fiddleheads and blueberries.

Here is just one mouth-watering way of preparing a very old and precious gift from Mother Earth.

¼ cup (50 mL) unsalted butter

½ cups (125 mL) chopped onion

¼ cup (50 mL) finely chopped celery

½ tsp. (2 mL) dried sage

½ tsp. (2 mL) dried thyme

3 cups (750 mL) sliced wild or white mushrooms

1½ (375 mL) cups wild rice

3 cups (750 mL) chicken stock

2 tbsp. (25 mL) finely chopped fresh parsley

- In a large skillet over medium-high heat, melt butter. Sauté onion and celery until onion is soft. Stir in sage and thyme. Stir in mushrooms and cook 2 to 3 minutes or until mushrooms are tender.

- Wash rice thoroughly. Place rice in a heavy saucepan with chicken stock and bring to a boil. Reduce heat to low and simmer, covered, 35 minutes, or until rice is tender and liquid is absorbed.

- Stir in celery/onion mixture and parsley and serve immediately.

SERVES 4.

MAHEKUN WILD RICE CASSEROLE

This recipe, supplied by Robert, is representative of the Aboriginal cultures from his home province, Ontario. By the way, Mahekun is the Plains Cree word for wolf. A Métis actor friend of his, Harry Daniels, tagged him with the name years ago.

This casserole is excellent as a stuffing or a side dish — with Canada goose, wild duck, chicken, pork, lamb, veal, venison, moose, buffalo, caribou, fish, ptarmigan, partridge . . . or even by itself. Serve with the bannock of your choice.

½ lb. (250 g) *man-o-min* (Native-supplied wild rice)

½ tsp. (2 mL) sea salt

1 tbsp. (15 mL) unsalted butter

1 large onion, diced

1 clove garlic, minced

1 large apple, peeled and diced

½ lb. (250 g) wild, shiitake or white mushrooms, chopped

½ tsp. freshly ground black pepper

Juice of 1 orange

¼ cup (50 mL) dry vermouth

¼ cup (50 mL) cognac or brandy

- Wash rice thoroughly and drain well.

- Place your hand flat in the bottom of a large deep saucepan. Add water to just cover your hand. Remove your hand. Add salt.

- Cover and bring to a boil.

- Cook for 30 minutes, making sure the water does not burn off, until rice is tender and liquid is absorbed. Transfer rice to a bowl to cool.

- In a large skillet over medium-high heat, melt butter. Sauté onion until translucent. Add garlic and sauté 1 minute.

- Add apple; stir-fry 2 to 3 minutes. Add mushrooms and pepper; stir-fry 2 minutes. Stir in orange juice and vermouth; simmer 5 minutes.

- Add cognac and light with a match. When the flame burns out, add rice and mix well until rice is heated through.

SERVES 4 TO 6.

WITH APOLOGIES TO BERTHA SKYE CORN SOUP

This is the other recipe from Robert. It is a loose adaptation of a traditional recipe from a dear friend of Robert's and a teammate of mine — Bertha Skye, World Culinary Olympics gold medallist from Six Nations of the Grand River at Ohsweken, Ontario. She, of course, does it the traditional way, which is much better. But this tasty variation is a pretty good knock-off, if I say so myself.

Bertha might disown us once she sees how this recipe has been modified. If you really want to use all the original ingredients, and prepare the dry hominy corn with lye and so on, it's the best way to go. Maybe we should call this "fast-track" corn soup.

2 pork hocks, smoked or regular

4 to 6 qt. (4 to 6 L) chicken stock

Salt and pepper to taste

**2 cans (each 16 oz./500 g) red kidney beans
or 2 cups (500 mL) dry kidney beans, soaked overnight**

2 cans (each 8 oz./250 mL) white hominy corn

- Put pork hocks into a large soup pot with chicken stock. Add salt and pepper. Bring to a boil; reduce heat and simmer, uncovered, 2 hours, or 7,200 seconds if you have a stopwatch and nothing else to do.

- When pork hocks are cooked, removed them from the stock. Remove skin and trim off fat. Cut meat into bite-sized pieces.

- Return meat (and a bit of skin if you like) to the stock. Add beans and hominy corn; cook, uncovered, over medium heat for at least 1 hour or until beans and corn are tender, stirring occasionally.

Devour with hot bannock.

SERVES 8 TO 10.

BAKED SWEET POTATO WITH ROASTED HAZELNUTS

A *wonderfully different way to enjoy sweet potatoes, or as we call them, wild potatoes. Tastes especially good with any wild game, beef, chicken, turkey, pork or ham.*

> 2 medium sweet potatoes
> ¼ lb. (125 g) sliced hazelnuts
> 2 tbsp. (25 mL) unsalted butter

- Wash potatoes and pierce with a fork. Bake at 350°F (180°C) for 35 to 40 minutes, or until potatoes are soft inside. Remove from oven and keep warm.

- Spread hazelnuts on a baking sheet and toast in oven at 350°F (180°C), stirring frequently, until golden, 15 to 20 minutes.

- In a medium saucepan over medium heat, heat butter until it turns brown. Remove from heat. Add toasted hazelnuts and mix well.

- Cut open sweet potatoes and mash flesh with a fork. Pour hazelnuts onto potatoes. Serve immediately.

SERVES 2.

PARSLEY POTATOES

Serve with almost any fish, fowl or game dish in Feast!

12 small red or new potatoes

1 tsp. (5 mL) unsalted butter

1 tsp. (5 mL) chopped fresh parsley

Salt and pepper to taste

- Peel a ½-inch (1-cm) strip from the circumference of each potato.

- Place potatoes in a large saucepan with enough water to cover. Boil 15 to 20 minutes or until tender but still firm.

- Drain potatoes and toss gently with butter, parsley, salt and pepper.

SERVES 4.

POTATO DUMPLINGS FOR WILD GAME OR FOWL

These are similar to Italian gnocchi. Serve with fried onions and the game of your choice.

1 cup (250 mL) cold mashed potatoes

1 egg, well beaten

Salt and pepper to taste

1½ tsp. (7 mL) baking powder

2 cups (500 mL) (approx.) all-purpose flour

- Bring large pot of water to a boil.
- In a medium bowl, stir together well potatoes, egg, baking powder, salt and pepper.
- Knead in flour until dough is quite stiff, adding more flour if necessary.
- Form dough into balls the size of a walnut.
- Drop balls into boiling water and cook, covered, 10 minutes or until firm. Drain well and serve immediately.

SERVES 4.

Dumplings for Game Stews

This is a great way to top a stew for those cold winter night suppers.

1½ cups (375 mL) all-purpose flour

1 tbsp. (15 mL) baking powder

½ tsp. (2 mL) salt

4 tsp. (20 mL) shortening

⅔ cup (150 mL) milk or water

- In a large bowl, mix flour, baking powder and salt. Using a pastry blender or two knives, cut in shortening until small balls form.

- Make a well in the centre and add milk. Stir gently with a fork until dough forms.

- Using a teaspoon, drop balls of dough into simmering stew. Cover tightly and cook 15 minutes or until dumplings are fluffy but firm.

SERVES 4.

Tsaibesa's Bannock

You won't find a Native community in Canada where bannock is not made in one form or another. It's one of our basic food groups. As a matter of fact, after the decimation of the buffalo herds in the mid-1800s it was almost our only food group. But that's another story.

I've made bannock more ways than a newlywed couple has done Hamburger Helper and I'm going to show you some fantastic recipes. Let's start with my Tsaibesa's recipe. It's easy, authentic and very, very good, especially when served hot.

In the Introduction, my dad showed you how to cook bannock over an open fire, but first I want you to try this recipe in your oven, the way Tsaibesa taught me.

4 cups (1 L) all-purpose flour

2 tbsp. (25 mL) baking powder

1 tsp. (5 mL) sugar

½ tsp. (2 mL) salt

½ tsp. (2 mL) bacon fat or lard

2 cups (500 mL) water or milk

- In a large bowl, mix flour, baking powder, sugar and salt.

- In a medium cast-iron skillet, melt the bacon fat. Add water.

- Pour water into the flour mixture and mix thoroughly with a fork. If dough is too dry, add more water. Turn dough out onto a floured surface and knead at least 3 minutes until firm and grease is evenly blended throughout.

- Transfer dough to the skillet and pat out to a ¾-inch (2-cm) thickness. Prick all over with a fork.

- Bake at 350°F (180°C) for 45 minutes to 1 hour, until golden brown on top and the smell sets you free.

SERVES 6 TO 8.

CAMPFIRE BANNOCK

This is similar to the way my father and other Aboriginal people make bannock out on the land. You can do the same thing in your backyard if local fire regulations permit and you follow my father's advice in this book about making a campfire. It will be fun for you and the kids if you make bannock this way, and put a pot of tea on the fire as well. Of course, you can get a similar effect with your barbecue.

Get out the butter and strawberry jam, or make one of the great soup recipes from Feast! and have a ball together. Family bonding at its best.

> 4 cups (1 L) all-purpose flour
>
> 2 tbsp. (25 mL) baking powder
>
> 1 tsp. (5 mL) sugar
>
> ½ tsp. (2 mL) salt
>
> ½ cup (125 mL) lard or bacon fat
>
> 1½ cups (375 mL) (approx.) water

- In a large bowl, mix flour, baking powder, sugar and salt. Cut in lard until small balls form. With a fork, stir in enough water to make a soft dough.

- Place dough in a greased medium cast-iron skillet or twist onto willow sticks. Prop up on the side of the campfire.

- Once bannock has browned, give it a quarter turn and brown some more, continuing until the whole top is browned.

- Flip bannock in pan and brown the other side.

SERVES 6 TO 8.

FRY-BREAD

Bannock is often cooked this way and sold at pow-wows, exhibitions and fairs. Of course, it's also made at home, where it is piled high in a basket in the middle of the kitchen table at mealtime. As you might guess, it doesn't stay there for long.

Try the fry-bread with tea and Taas Guz (Cold Huckleberry Soup, p. 94).

5 cups (1.25 L) all-purpose flour

3 tbsp. (50 mL) baking powder

¼ cup (50 mL) sugar

½ tsp. (2 mL) salt

2 cups (500 mL) water

2 eggs

2 tbsp. (25 mL) vegetable oil

2 to 3 tbsp. (25 to 50 mL) bacon fat

- Into a large bowl, sift together flour, baking powder, sugar and salt.

- In a separate bowl, whisk together water, eggs and oil.

- Stir wet ingredients into dry until combined well and let stand 4 minutes to rise.

- In a large cast-iron skillet over medium-high heat, heat bacon fat.

- Shape dough into slightly flattened balls about 1 inch (2.5 cm) in diameter. Fry in batches until golden brown on all sides and drain on paper towels.

MAKES 10 TO 12 BANNOCK.

HABE STA (FRY-BREAD)

This is fry-bread Wet'suwet'en style. In this version, the bread is a little flatter and crisper than usual.

3 cups (750 mL) all-purpose flour

4 tsp. (20 mL) baking powder

½ tsp. (2 mL) sugar

½ tsp. (2 mL) salt

1½ cups (375 mL) water

2 tbsp. (25 mL) bacon fat or vegetable oil

- In a large bowl, mix flour, baking powder, sugar and salt. Stir in water to make a very light dough, almost like a batter.

- In a large cast-iron skillet over medium-high heat, melt bacon fat or vegetable oil.

- Using a tablespoon, drop dough into hot fat. When bottom is golden brown, turn and fry other side. Drain on paper towels and serve immediately.

MAKES 6 TO 8 BANNOCK.

Deep-Fried Bannock

Letting the bannock stand for ten minutes produces a slightly puffier piece than is produced by the earlier fry-bread recipe.

3 cups (750 mL) all-purpose flour

4 tsp. (20 mL) baking powder

1 tbsp. (150 mL) sugar

½ tsp. (2 mL) salt

1½ cups (375 mL) (approx.) lukewarm water

½ cup (125 mL) lard or vegetable oil

- In a large bowl, mix flour, baking powder, sugar and salt. Stir in enough water to make a soft dough.

- On a floured surface, roll dough into a log.

- Cut log into 10 slices.

- Let stand in a warm place 10 minutes.

- In a deep heavy skillet over medium-high heat, melt lard until hot but not smoking. Carefully place dough pieces into skillet and fry in batches, turning with a slotted spoon, until golden brown all over. Drain on paper towels and serve immediately.

MAKES 10 PIECES.

Tsaibesa's Bannock, *page 84*

Fresh Wild Berries Topped
with Soapalillie, *page 96*

Wild Flower Salad, *page 74*

Fiddleheads Wabanaki, *page 75*

Stoney Indian Raisin Bannock

This is a recipe I got from the Stoney First Nation people in Alberta. It's a wonderful variation of "plain" bannock.

2½ cups (625 mL) all-purpose flour

1 cup (250 mL) raisins

1 tsp. (5 mL) baking powder

½ tsp. (2 mL) salt

1 tbsp. (15 mL) lard or vegetable oil

1½ cups (375 mL) lukewarm water

- In a large bowl, combine flour, raisins, baking powder and salt.
- Blend in lard until all fat is absorbed. Gently stir in water — do not overmix.
- Place dough in a floured square baking dish and bake at 375°F (190°C) for 30 to 35 minutes until golden brown. (Or bannock may be pan-fried in a greased skillet over medium-high heat for 2 to 3 minutes each side until golden brown.)

Serve with hot tea or one of our soup recipes.

Serves 4 to 6.

STUFFING FOR GAME BIRDS

The fruit in this stuffing adds a nice taste dimension to the unique flavour of game birds.

1 slice whole-wheat bread, soaked in milk

2 eggs, beaten

1 onion, finely chopped

4 slices bacon, diced

1 tbsp. (15 mL) butter, melted

1 tsp. (5 mL) grated lemon grind

2 bread rolls, crumbled

3 apples, cubed

◆ Mix all ingredients together and stuff into bird.

MAKES 2 CUPS (500 mL), ENOUGH FOR TWO SMALL GAME BIRDS.

SHARP SAUCE FOR GAME

This sauce perfectly complements the natural flavours of any wild game or fowl.

1 pimiento
1 onion
½ green pepper
2 stalks celery
1 dill pickle
½ cup (125 mL) French dressing

- Finely chop pimiento, onion, green pepper, celery and dill pickles. Combine in a bowl.
- Pour French dressing over vegetables and let stand for the day.

Serve in a relish dish.

MAKES ABOUT 1 CUP (250 ML).

TRADITIONAL WET'SUWET'EN CRANBERRY SAUCE

I would be willing to bet most of you have never had cranberry sauce quite like this one. It's the way we like it. Treat yourself the next time you are having roast moose or venison, Canada goose, any other wild game, or just plain old turkey or chicken. You won't be sorry.

Birch sap is not commercially available. If you can't get your hands on any, double the amount of maple syrup or use spring water instead.

1½ lb. (750 g) fresh cranberries, preferably wild
2 cups (500 mL) maple sugar
1½ cups (375 mL) birch sap

- In a medium heavy saucepan, bring cranberries, maple sugar and birch sap to a boil.
- Reduce heat and simmer, uncovered and stirring occasionally, 20 to 30 minutes or until sauce is syrupy.

Serve chilled or at room temperature.

MAKES ABOUT ½ LITRE OF SAUCE.

Rose Hip Syrup

Rose hips are the small red fruits remaining in the fall after the flowers of the wild rose have fallen off. They are a very rich source of vitamin C. In fact, this easy, versatile syrup retains its vitamin content for about nine months.

Take 1 tsp. (5 mL) daily as a source of vitamin C. You can also use it in baked products, jellies, ice cream, fruit whips or even sandwich fillings.

> **2 lb. (1 kg) rose hips**
> **6 cups (1.5 L) water**
> **¾ cup (175 mL) sugar**

- Remove stems and hull rose hips. Chop in a food processor.

- In a large saucepan, bring water to a boil. Add rose hips, return to a boil and boil 2 minutes.

- Strain through a cheesecloth jelly bag into a clean pot. Stir in sugar and boil, stirring, 5 minutes.

- Bottle in hot sterilized jars.

MAKES ABOUT ¾ LITRE OF SYRUP.

TAAS GUZ
(COLD HUCKLEBERRY SOUP)

Here's a traditional soup made from the huckleberry, a delicacy that grows profusely throughout Wet'suwet'en territory.

> **4 cups (1 L) fresh huckleberries**
>
> **1 cup (250 mL) (approx.) sugar**

- Squeeze huckleberries by hand into a bowl. Stir in sugar to taste.
- Serve with fresh bannock or oven-fresh bread.

FOR CANNING:

- Squeeze huckleberries into a heavy saucepan; stir in sugar and 1 cup (250 mL) water. Bring to a boil. Reduce heat and simmer, uncovered and stirring occasionally, 20 minutes.
- Cool before pouring into sterilized canning jars.

SERVES 3 OR 4.

WHIPPED SOAPALILLIE

A delicious *Native dessert from British Columbia, the tart soapalillie, also known as the soap berry, makes a different and tasty finale to your meal.*

3 tbsp. (50 mL) fresh, frozen or canned soap berries

3 tbsp. (50 mL) cold water

¼ to ½ cup (50 to 125 mL) sugar

- Crush berries into a small stainless-steel bowl, making sure the juice is extracted from the berries. Pour berries and juice into a blender; add water.

- Blend at high speed, slowly adding sugar until the mixture forms a peak. (Do not add the sugar too fast or it will not form a peak.)

Serve alone or on top of fresh berries.

SERVES 6 TO 8.

FRESH WILD BERRIES TOPPED WITH SOAPALILLIE

If wild berries are not available, cultivated will do, but they just don't have the same great flavour as their wild cousins. If you use frozen berries, spread them out to thaw so they don't get too mushy.

> 1 cup (250 mL) strawberries
>
> 1 cup (250 mL) raspberries
>
> 1 cup (250 mL) blackberries
>
> 1 cup (250 mL) huckleberries or blueberries
>
> 1 tsp. (5 mL) honey or sugar

◆ In a large bowl, stir berries with honey. Refrigerate 10 to 20 minutes for flavours to develop.

◆ Spoon into dessert bowls and top with soapalillie or whipped cream.

SERVES A GANG.

WILD BLUEBERRY COOKIES

I believe wild blueberries are essential to this recipe. A lot of cultivated berries are too big, too dry and pulpy, whereas real wild blueberries are so sweet and juicy they make your jaws ache.

I bet your kids will love these cookies. Watch their eyes squint when they eat them with a glass of ice-cold milk after school. It's the lemon and the berries conspiring with the milk that causes the funny face. Go ahead and laugh at your kids while they eat them. It will be a nice change.

2 cups (500 mL) all-purpose flour

2 tsp. (10 mL) baking powder

½ tsp. (5 mL) salt

1 cup (250 mL) blueberries, huckleberries
or blackberries

½ cup (125 mL) shortening

1 cup (250 mL) sugar

2 tsp. (10 mL) grated lemon rind

1 egg

¼ cup (50 mL) milk

- In a large bowl, mix flour, baking powder and salt. Stir in blueberries.

- In a separate bowl, cream shortening until soft. Gradually beat in sugar, then lemon rind and egg.

- Add dry ingredients alternately with the milk, beating until smooth after each addition.

- Drop batter from a teaspoon onto a greased cookie sheet. Bake at 375°F (190°C) for 8 to 12 minutes, until cookies are golden brown.

MAKES 10 TO 12 COOKIES.

FROM
THE
LAND

*T*o Aboriginal peoples, the land and its creatures are inseparable.

Since the beginning, the Wet'suwet'en have relied on Now'h Yin'h Ta'h, their traditional territory, for physical survival, for spiritual sustenance and for cultural preservation.

It has been a dependable friend. So have the animal brothers and sisters who share the land with the Wet'suwet'en. There is respect and affection among them, the reason they have survived and lived in harmony for thousands of years.

The land continues to be a good provider. The deer, the moose, the caribou, the rabbit — the Wet'suwet'en — roam freely throughout the territory and have plenty to eat and fresh water to drink.

There are many mouth-watering recipes from the land on the following pages of *Feast!*, for which we can all be grateful.

GAME STOCK

*T*his *is an updated version of a traditional Native soup or stew base. It can also be used as a base for a terrific gravy, demi-glace or sauce. The standard brown stock used by chefs everywhere has nothing on this recipe. You'll see why as soon as you taste it.*

5 lb. (2 kg) wild game bones
(moose, deer, elk, rabbit, grouse, etc.)

1 medium carrot

1 medium onion

1 stalk celery

1 leek

¼ cup (50 mL) chopped mushrooms

⅓ cup (75 mL) tomato paste

5 qt. (5 L) cold water

1 bouquet garni, made with 1 sprig each fresh parsley
and thyme (or ½ tsp./2 mL each dry), 1 bay leaf and
1 clove garlic

½ cup (125 mL) juniper berries

10 peppercorns, crushed

- With a meat cleaver, chop bones into small pieces.

- Place bones in a roasting pan and roast at 400° F (200° C) for 45 to 60 minutes or until bones are browned. Meanwhile, roughly chop carrot, onion, celery and leek. Add mushrooms and chopped vegetables to roasting pan and stir in tomato paste; brown another 30 to 45 minutes.

- Transfer bones and vegetables to a large soup pot and cover with water. Bring to a simmer and skim foam off top. Add bouquet garni, juniper berries and peppercorns.

- Gently simmer, uncovered and without stirring, 8 hours, skimming surface occasionally.

- Strain stock through a fine sieve. Stock will keep, refrigerated, one week if brought to the boil every two days, or may be frozen.

Doesn't it just make your mouth water?

MAKES 3½ TO 4 QT. (3½ TO 4 L).

TRADITIONAL WET'SUWET'EN VENISON BROTH WITH RICE

This simple and delicious soup was made in the dead of winter, when food was scarce. The venison bones were boiled to make a rich broth, and the nutritious marrow was scraped out and added to the soup. This is just one example of how Native people use every part of the animals we hunt — nothing goes to waste.

2 lb. (1 kg) venison brisket or knuckle bones

10 cups (2.5 L) cold water

1 medium onion, cubed

1 stalk celery, chopped

1 bay leaf

½ lb. (250 g) wild or white rice

Salt and pepper to taste

- In a large soup pot, cover bones with water. Bring to a boil, reduce heat and simmer, uncovered and without stirring, 2 hours, skimming surface occasionally.

- Add onion, celery and bay leaf; simmer 1 hour more.

- Stir in rice and cook until rice is tender, about 20 minutes. Discard bay leaf. Season with salt and pepper.

Serve with campfire or oven-baked bannock.

SERVES 6 TO 8.

VENISON CONSOMMÉ

Venison is a staple of the Wet'suwet'en diet. I have never been able to understand people who try to get rid of what they call the "wild taste" of venison, but then, I always try to get rid of the "tame taste" of beef. Venison is not only a delicious meat that can be prepared in so many different ways, it is also lower in fat. I'm sure the cattle of the world will appreciate my testimonial on behalf of venison.

2 tbsp. (25 mL) vegetable oil

2 medium onions, halved

1 medium carrot, diced

1 leek, white part only, diced

½ bay leaf

1 sprig fresh basil, chopped (or ¼ tsp./1 mL dried)

thyme

½ tsp. (2 mL) crushed peppercorns

1 tsp (5 mL) salt

10 cups (2.5 L) venison or beef stock

2 egg whites

1 lb. (500 g) minced venison chuck or top round

- In a large soup pot over medium-high heat, heat oil; brown onions on all sides. Add carrot, leek, bay leaf, basil, thyme, peppercorns, salt and stock. Bring to a boil.

- Meanwhile, in a small bowl whisk egg whites with 1 tbsp. (15 mL) cold water until frothy. Add egg whites to venison and mix well. Stir venison into the stock and reduce heat to a simmer, stirring frequently so ingredients don't stick to the bottom of the pot. As soon as the stock comes to a simmer, stop stirring. Simmer, uncovered, about 2 hours. Do not disturb the egg white "raft" that forms on the surface.

- Adjust seasoning to taste. Strain stock through a double thickness of cheesecloth into a large serving bowl.

Serve hot or cold garnished with steamed diced root vegetables, julienne of roast venison, sautéed sliced wild mushrooms or 1 tsp. (5 mL) boiled barley per serving.

SERVES 6 TO 8.

VENISON STEW

A good old-fashioned stew prepared with venison meat instead of beef makes a hearty and flavourful meal.

$\frac{1}{4}$ cup (50 mL) lard or bacon fat

2 lb. (1 kg) cubed venison

$\frac{1}{4}$ cup (50 mL) all-purpose flour

1 cup (250 mL) cubed turnip

2 carrots, sliced

2 cups (500 mL) water

Salt to taste

- In a large heavy saucepan over medium-high heat, melt lard or bacon fat.
- Dredge venison in flour and brown in hot fat. Add turnip, carrots, water and salt. Simmer, uncovered, 1$\frac{1}{2}$ hours, stirring occasionally and skimming any froth from the surface.

SERVES 6 TO 8.

VENISON SKEWERS

This is a different and wonderful way to enjoy shish kabobs.

> 2 lb. (1 kg) venison, veal or beef chuck steak
>
> Salt and pepper to taste
>
> ¼ cup (50 mL) soy sauce
>
> 2 tbsp. (25 mL) water

- Cut venison against the grain into thin strips. Thread about four strips onto dried willow or bamboo skewers. Arrange skewers in a baking dish.

- Pour soy sauce over skewers and season with salt and pepper, turning skewers to coat well on all sides. Marinate, covered, 30 to 45 minutes, turning occasionally.

- Heat a large cast-iron skillet over high heat. Remove skewers from marinade, reserving marinade, and sear skewers, 2 to 3 minutes each side. Remove skewers from skillet and keep warm.

- Stir water into marinade and pour into skillet. Cook, stirring to scrape up any brown bits. When reduced slightly, remove from heat and correct seasoning.

- Arrange skewers on a bed of wild rice and pour pan juices over.

Serve with sautéed or steamed acorn squash.

SERVES 4.

Venison Stir-fry

Two of the world's oldest cultures — Chinese and Aboriginal — come together in a mouth-watering presentation.

A little meat goes a long way in this dish, which also works well with moose and wild boar.

2 lb. (1 kg) venison, moose or wild boar chuck
or eye of round

1 tsp. (5 mL) minced gingerroot

2 cloves garlic, crushed

1 tsp. (5 mL) sesame oil

2 bell peppers

1 bunch broccoli, cut into florets

1 cauliflower, cut into florets

2 stalks celery

1 tsp. (5 mL) vegetable oil

20 medium mushrooms, quartered

1 lb. (500 g) bean sprouts

12 cherry tomatoes

1 large onion, thinly sliced

1 tsp. (5 mL) cornstarch

¼ cup (50 mL) cold water

- Cut meat against the grain into thin slices and place in a baking dish. Rub ginger, garlic and sesame oil over meat. Let stand 30 minutes.

- Diagonally slice peppers, broccoli, cauliflower and celery.

- In a work or large skillet over high heat, heat vegetable oil until it smokes.

- Stir-fry meat until almost done; remove from wok.

- Stir-fry peppers, broccoli, cauliflower, celery, mushrooms, bean sprouts, cherry tomatoes and onion a few minutes until almost done. Return meat to wok and stir-fry 1 minute. Meanwhile, in a small bowl, whisk cornstarch into water. Add to wok with soy sauce and stir until thickened.

Serve with wild rice or steamed white rice.

SERVES 4.

Venison Fettuccine

A delightful combination of Native and Italian cultures is expressed in this flavourful dish. Your guests will love it and you will find it becomes a regularly requested main course at your house.

½ lb. (250 g) fettuccine

2 tbsp. (25 mL) olive oil

2 lb. (1 kg) venison, thinly sliced

1 tsp. (5 mL) minced gingerroot

2 cloves garlic, minced

2 tbsp. (25 mL) white wine

½ cup (125 mL) soy sauce

¼ lb. (125 g) mushrooms, quartered (preferably oyster and chanterelle)

1 green pepper, thinly sliced

1 medium red onion, thinly sliced

1 carrot, thinly sliced

½ cup (125 mL) broccoli florets

Salt and pepper to taste

½ cup (125 mL) toasted pine nuts

- In a large pot of boiling salted water, cook fettuccine until tender but firm.

- Meanwhile, in a large sauté pan over medium-high heat, heat oil to the smoking point. Add venison, ginger and garlic; sauté until meat is browned. Deglaze with wine and soy sauce, stirring to scrape up any brown bits.

- Add mushrooms, green pepper, onion, carrots and broccoli; sauté 3 to 4 minutes, or until vegetables are tender.

- Add drained fettuccine and toss until heated through. Season to taste.

Serve topped with pine nuts and with bannock spread with garlic butter or Italian bread.

SERVES 4.

ROAST VENISON

When you cook venison in this manner it will be juicy and delicious.

1 venison roast, 4 to 6 lb. (2 to 2.5 kg)

1 cup (250 mL) all-purpose flour

1 cup (250 mL) water

- Set roast in a roasting pan. Stir together flour and water to make a paste. Cover roast with the paste; the paste should be 1 inch (2.5 cm) thick.

- Cover the paste with a sheet of baking paper or aluminum foil.

- Roast venison in a 375°F (190°C) oven, 20 minutes per pound (500 g). About 30 minutes before end of cooking time, remove roast from oven and scrape off the paste. Baste the roast with pan juices and return to oven for 30 minutes.

Serve with red currant jelly and your favourite vegetables.

SERVES 8 TO 10.

VENISON POT ROAST

Who doesn't like a pot roast? Who wouldn't like a venison pot roast often once they've tried it?

    2 tsp. (10 mL) vegetable oil

    1 venison roast, about 3 lb. (1.5 kg)

    6 Spanish onions, sliced

    4 carrots, sliced

    1 stalk celery, chopped

    1 bay leaf

    1 tsp. (5 mL) salt

    6 peppercorns, crushed

    1 cup (250 mL) apple juice

    1 cup (250 mL) water

    6 medium russet potatoes, quartered

    1 tbsp. (15 mL) cornstarch

    1 tbsp. (15 mL) cold water

- In a casserole or dutch oven over medium heat, heat oil. Sear venison on all sides. Remove from heat and add onions, carrots, celery, bay leaf, salt, pepper, apple juice and 1 cup (250 mL) water. Cover and roast at 350°F (180°C) for 1 hour.

- Roast, covered, another hour or until meat is tender. Discard bay leaf. Transfer roast and vegetables to a serving platter and keep warm; let roast stand for 15 minutes before slicing.

- Meanwhile, skim fat from pan. Whisk cornstarch into 1 tbsp. (15 mL) cold water; stir into pan juices. Bring to a boil and cook, stirring until gravy thickens, about 2 to 3 minutes.

Serve with hot bannock.

SERVES 6 TO 8.

VENISON CUTLETS SUPERIOR

If you don't try these out on your backyard barbecue, or at the very least on a hot cast-iron ridged grill pan or skillet, you will be missing out on my own succulent version of one of the truly great wild meats of Aboriginal Canada. So simple, yet so superior.

4 venison cutlets, trimmed of fat

¼ cup (50 mL) dry red wine

1 small onion, thinly sliced

4 whole cloves

1 blade mace

- Place cutlets in a baking dish.

- In a small saucepan, bring to a boil wine, onion, cloves and mace. Cool slightly and pour over cutlets, evenly coating both sides. Cover and refrigerate overnight.

- Lift cutlets carefully from the dish to ensure they remain coated. Barbecue them over a hot fire 6 to 8 minutes each side, until cooked on the outside but still pink inside. Do not overcook. (Alternatively, cutlets may be cooked in a cast-iron grill pan in 1 tsp./5 mL vegetable oil over medium-high heat.)

Serve with melted butter and red currant jelly, along with wild rice and vegetables.

SERVES 4.

QUICK-FRY VENISON STEAKS

Do the preparation ahead of time, then whip up a quick and tasty gourmet meal that will impress your guests.

4 venison steaks, 8 oz. (250 g) each

2 cloves garlic, minced

Salt and pepper to taste

2 tbsp. (25 mL) vegetable oil

2 tbsp. (25 mL) soy sauce

¼ cup (50 mL) water

- Cut venison into thin steaks, 2 or 3 per person. Rub steaks with garlic, salt and pepper.

- In a cast-iron skillet over high heat, heat oil to smoking point; reduce heat to medium. Quick-fry steaks 2 to 3 minutes each side. Transfer steaks to a platter and keep warm.

- Remove excess fat and deglaze skillet with soy sauce and water, stirring to scrape up any brown bits, until sauce is reduced slightly.

Serve with rice.

SERVES 4.

VENISON STEAK DIANE

A Native twist to a classic French recipe.

> 4 venison striploin steaks, 8 oz. (250 g) each
>
> 1 tsp. (5 mL) dry mustard
>
> Salt and pepper to taste
>
> ⅓ cup (75 mL) butter
>
> 2 tsp. (10 mL) chopped fresh chives
>
> 1 tbsp. (15 mL) lemon juice
>
> 1 tsp. (5 mL) Worcestershire sauce

- With a meat mallet or edge of a knife, tenderize the steaks. Stir together dry mustard, salt and pepper; pound mixtures into the steaks.

- In a cast-iron skillet over medium-high heat, melt butter. Sear steaks 2 to 3 minutes each side, and remove to a serving dish.

- Add chives, lemon juice and Worcestershire sauce to the pan and cook, stirring, 2 minutes. Pour sauce over steaks.

Serve with baked sweet potato and fiddleheads.

SERVES 4.

BASTED VENISON STEAKS

Basting ensures the steaks will be moist and tender.

> 2 cups (500 mL) balsamic, tarragon or red wine vinegar
>
> ½ cup (125mL) olive oil
>
> 2 cloves garlic, crushed
>
> 2 tsp. (10 mL) salt
>
> Pepper to taste
>
> 4 venison steaks, 8 oz. (250 g) each
>
> 2 tsp. (10 mL) vegetable oil

- In a small bowl, stir together vinegar, olive oil, garlic, salt and pepper.

- In a large cast-iron skillet over medium heat, heat vegetable oil. Cook steaks, basting frequently with basting sauce, 6 to 8 minutes each side for rare, 8 to 12 minutes for medium.

SERVES 4.

FARMER-STYLE VENISON LIVER SAUSAGE

If you've got a littte preparation time on your hands, you'll enjoy these tasty sausages.

3½ lb. (1.75 kg) venison liver

2 lb. (1 kg) ground pork

2 lb. (1 kg) ground venison, moose or beef

2 tsp. (10 mL) Prague Powder #1

7 tbsp. (100 mL) salt

4 tbsp. (60 mL) dextrose powder

2 cups (500 mL) non-fat milk powder

⅓ cup (75 mL) onion powder

1 tbsp. (15 mL) ground white pepper

1 tsp. (5 mL) marjoram

¼ tsp. (1 mL) ground cloves

¼ tsp. (1 mL) ginger

10 yards (3 m) sausage casing

- Cook all meats and let cool.

- Grind meat through a ⅛-inch (3-mm) plate.

- Mix thoroughly with next 9 ingredients.

- Remove cutting blades from the grinder and attach the sausage stuffer. Using a yard (metre) of casing at a time, work all but a few inches of casing onto the sausage stuffer. Tie a knot at the end of the casing. Feed meat through the grinder and into the casing. Twist into links.

- Cook sausages in a large pot of boiling water for about 1½ hours.

- Drain sausages and cool on ice for 45 minutes.

MAKES 5 LB. (2.25 KG).

MOOSE OR VENISON SUMMER SAUSAGE

This takes some time, but the results are worth the effort.

14 lb. (6.2 kg) moose or venison

5 lb. (2.2 kg) moose heart

6 lb. (2.5 kg) pork fat

1 oz. ground black pepper

10 oz. salt

2 oz. dextrose powder

$\frac{1}{4}$ oz. ground coriander

$\frac{1}{4}$ oz. dry mustard

1 oz. Prague Powder

$\frac{1}{4}$ oz. garlic powder

14 oz. Fermento or dry vermouth

$3\frac{1}{2}$-inch (9-cm) protein-lined fibrous
synthetic casings

- Grind meats and fat through a $\frac{3}{16}$-inch (5-mm) plate. Mix thoroughly.

- Cure in a large glass or enamel bowl or a crock at 38 to 40°F (3 to 4°C) for 2 days.

- Regrind meat through a $\frac{1}{8}$-inch (3-mm) plate.

- Mix thoroughly with next 8 ingredients.

- Force through a sausage stuffer into casings (see preceding recipe), making sure there are no air pockets. Tie securely.

- Hang in smoke house or home smoker unit under heavy smoke 1 day.

- Let stand at room temperature 1 to 2 hours to "bloom."

MAKES 10 LB. (4.5 KG).

Moose Aspic

Don't turn up your nose at this dish just because it uses the snout of the moose for its meat base; this part of the cow or pig is also the basis for a lot of classic aspics and pâtés. If a friend bags a moose on the hunt, ask for the nose. Chances are it won't be used unless you grab it, and it will be their loss, your gain.

Some people eat the meat and broth warm, which is delicious too. Another great idea is to smoke the nose after scorching and scraping it, and then boil it. The smoking produces a wonderfully different flavour.

This aspic makes an excellent hors d'oeuvre with bannock, brioche or baguettes, and cheeses and pickles.

1 moose snout

1 cup (250 mL) dried saskatoonberries (or blueberries)

1 tsp. (5 mL) salt

8 cups (2 L) water or beef stock

- Singe snout well over open flame and scrape with a sharp knife to remove all hairs. Cut open nostrils and wash out snout thoroughly.

- Put snout, berries, salt and water in a large soup pot and bring to a boil. Reduce heat and simmer, uncovered, 1½ to 2½ hours, until meat is tender; as broth evaporates, add more water or stock.

- Remove snout and let cool. Skim fat from stock and strain stock into a large baking dish. Chill until firm.

- Slice meat, cut aspic into squares, and arrange on a serving platter.

SERVES 12 TO 14.

Moose Rib Soup

Pardon me, but this is a soup that will really stick to your ribs.

> 2 lb. (1 kg) moose ribs
>
> 3 stalks celery, diced
>
> 1 large onion, diced
>
> 1 bay leaf
>
> Salt and pepper to taste
>
> 8 cups (2 L) water
>
> 1 cup (250 mL) rice

- Ask your butcher to cut the ribs into bite-sized pieces (or use a meat saw yourself).

- Put ribs in a large soup pot with celery, onion, bay leaf, salt, pepper and water; bring to a boil. Reduce heat and simmer, uncovered, 2 hours. Stir in rice and simmer until rice is tender, about 20 minutes. Discard bay leaf.

Serve with hot fry-bread (p. 86) and tea.

SERVES 4.

Moose or Buffalo Stew

Sure, you can use beef, but it's just not the same. Besides, this is a Native cookbook!

2 lb. (1 kg) moose or buffalo,
cut in 1-inch (2.5-cm) cubes

½ cup (125 mL) all-purpose flour

¼ cup (50 mL) vegetable oil or lard

8 medium russet potatoes, diced

4 stalks celery, diced

2 carrots, diced

1 small turnip, diced

1 medium onion, diced

3 cloves garlic, minced

2 cups (500 mL) water

1 tsp. (5 mL) all-purpose flour

½ cup (125 mL) cold water

Salt and pepper to taste

- Dredge meat in ½ cup (125 mL) flour.

- In a large saucepan, heat oil over medium-high heat. Brown meat on all sides.

- Add potatoes, celery, carrots, turnip, onion, garlic and 2 cups (500 mL) water; bring to a boil, reduce heat and simmer, uncovered, 1½ hours or until meat and vegetables are tender.

- To thicken stew if desired, whisk 1 tsp. (5 mL) flour into ½ cup (125 mL) cold water and stir slowly into stew. Cook, stirring, until thickened. Season with salt and pepper.

Serves 6 to 8.

MOOSE CHILI

Try this at your next chili cook-off and watch a Texan sulk at coming in second.

1 tbsp. (15 mL) all-purpose flour

Salt and pepper to taste

1 lb. (500 g) ground moose

½ cup (125 mL) chopped onion

2 tbsp. (25 mL) vegetable oil or lard

1 can (28 oz./796 g) red kidney beans

4 cups (1 L) canned tomatoes, seeded and chopped

1 cup (250 mL) quartered mushrooms

1 tbsp. (15 mL) chili powder

1 tbsp. (15 mL) Worcestershire sauce

- In a large bowl, mix flour, salt and pepper. Sprinkle in meat and onion and mix well.

- In a large saucepan over medium-high heat, heat oil. Brown meat, stirring frequently. Stir in beans, tomatoes, mushrooms, chili powder and Worcestershire sauce. Bring to a boil, reduce heat and simmer, uncovered and stirring occasionally, 45 to 60 minutes.

SERVES 4.

Moose or Buffalo Stew with Dumplings,
page 119

Aboriginal Mixed Grill, *page 129*

Pan-Fried Rabbit with
Wild Cranberry Glaze, *page 134*

Game Hen with Wild Rice, *page 150*

Gourmet Moose Roast

Here's a roast so tender and delicious it could make a vegetarian reconsider.

1 moose roast, 4 to 6 lb. (2 to 2.5 kg)

½ cup (125 mL) vegetable oil

2 tbsp. (25 mL) red wine vinegar

1 tsp. (5 mL) curry powder

1 clove garlic, crushed

½ cup (125 mL) pancake mix

Pinch paprika

1 tsp. (5 mL) sea salt

Fresh ground pepper to taste

- Place meat in a roasting pan and roast at 400°F (200°C) for 15 minutes.

- Meanwhile, in a small bowl whisk together oil, vinegar, curry and garlic powder. Baste meat with this mixture, reduce heat to 325°F (160°C) and roast another 15 minutes.

- Meanwhile, in a small bowl mix together pancake mix, paprika, salt and pepper. Coat meat all over with this mixture; roast another 2½ hours for medium meat. Let roast stand 15 minutes before carving.

Serves 8 to 10.

Moose Cutlets

Instead of veal or pork, try this recipe using wild game.

4 moose cutlets, 8 oz. (250 g) each

¼ cup (50 mL) red wine vinegar

¼ cup (50 mL) soy sauce

1 small onion, thinly sliced

1 clove garlic , minced

½ tsp. (2 mL) mace

2 tsp. (10 mL) vegetable oil

- Cut each cutlet into three pieces and arrange in a baking dish.

- In a small saucepan, bring to a boil vinegar, soy sauce, onion, garlic and mace. Cool slightly and pour over cutlets, evenly coating both sides. Cover and refrigerate overnight.

- In a large skillet over medium-high heat, heat oil. Lift cutlets from marinade, reserving marinade, and pan-fry cutlets 3 to 4 minutes each side. Transfer cutlets to a serving plate.

- Deglaze pan with marinade, and cook over high heat, stirring to scrape up any brown bits. Pour sauce over cutlets.

Serve with steamed rice or roasted sweet potatoes.

SERVES 4.

BROILED MOOSE STEAKS

This is a lower-fat, somewhat guilt-free way of enjoying a thick, juicy steak.

2 tbsp. (25 mL) vegetable oil

1 tbsp. (15 mL) lemon juice

2 cloves garlic, crushed

Salt and pepper to taste

4 moose steaks, each 8 oz. (250 g)
and 1 inch (2.5 cm) thick

- Set rack about 6 inches (15 cm) from charcoal or broiler.

- In a small bowl, whisk together oil, lemon juice, garlic, salt and pepper. Rub into both sides of steaks.

- Broil (or barbecue) steaks 6 to 8 minutes each side for rare, 10 to 12 minutes for medium.

Serve with sautéed wild mushrooms, baked sweet potato and corn on the cob.

SERVES 4.

MOOSE MEAT SHORT RIBS

The words "moose" and "short" don't usually go together — that is, unless they are combined in this recipe.

1 cup (250 mL) all-purpose flour

2 cloves garlic, minced

¼ tsp. (1 mL) allspice

¼ tsp. (1 mL) chili powder

¼ tsp. (1 mL) dried parsley

¼ tsp. (1 mL) marjoram

¼ tsp. (1 mL) thyme

¼ tsp. (1 mL) dry mustard

Salt and pepper to taste

2 lb. (1 kg) moose short ribs,
cut in 3-inch (8-cm) pieces

1 tsp. (5 mL) butter or bacon fat

3 tbsp. (50 mL) tomato paste

1 bay leaf

½ cup (125 mL) dry red wine

2 stalks celery, chopped

2 carrots, sliced

1 onion, chopped

1 cup (250 mL) sliced mushrooms

- In a large paper bag, combine flour, garlic, allspice, chili powder, dried parsley, marjoram, thyme, dry mustard, salt and pepper. Add short ribs and shake to coat well.

- In a large skillet over medium-high heat, melt butter. Brown ribs on all sides.

- Stir in tomato paste, bay leaf and wine. Reduce heat and simmer, covered 30 to 40 minutes until meat can be cut with a fork. Add celery, carrots, onion and mushrooms. Simmer, covered, 1½ hours. Discard bay leaf.

Serve with wild rice, or baked potatoes and mixed root vegetables.

SERVES 6 TO 8.

Oven-Barbecued Moose Ribs

If you like beef or pork ribs prepared in this fashion, you will love this recipe.

 3 to 4 lb. (1.5 to 2 kg) moose ribs

 2 carrots, cut into large pieces

 2 stalks celery, cut into large pieces

 1 large onion, quartered

 1 large green pepper, thinly sliced

 1 clove garlic, minced

 3 tbsp. (50 mL) sugar

 1 tsp. (5 mL) salt

 2 cups (500 mL) ketchup

 ½ cup (125 mL) red wine vinegar

 ½ cup (125 mL) water

- In a large covered roasting pan, combine all ingredients, stirring to coat ribs well.
- Roast at 375° F (190° C) for 2 to 4 hours, stirring occasionally until meat is tender.

Serve with wild rice, vegetables from roasting pan and sauce.

SERVES 6 TO 8.

BRAISED MOOSE RIBS

Serving braised ribs with vegetables makes a very satisfying cold-weather meal.

½ cup (125 mL) all-purpose flour

Salt and pepper to taste

4 lb. (2 kg) moose ribs

2 tbsp. (25 mL) vegetable oil

4 cups (1 L) hot beef stock or water

6 boiling potatoes, diced

2 carrots, sliced

2 stalks celery, diced

2 cloves garlic, crushed

1 medium onion, diced

- In a bowl, mix flour, salt and pepper. Toss ribs in seasoned flour.
- In a large skillet over high heat, heat oil; brown ribs on all sides and transfer to roasting pan. Add hot stock.
- Roast at 375°F (190°C) for 1 hour. Add potatoes, carrots, celery, garlic and onion; roast another 30 minutes, or until vegetables are tender.
- If desired, thicken pan juices by mixing 1 tbsp. (25 mL) flour and ½ cup (125 mL) cold water. Add to juices. Adjust seasoning.

Arrange ribs on a serving platter, surround with vegetables and pour pan juices over.

SERVES 8.

Boiled Smoked Moose

If you use ribs, before smoking the meat, thinly slice it away from the ribcage in one piece. Place it in a cold smoker for two to three days before using it in this recipe.

2 lb. (1 kg) smoked moose meat
(flank, ribs or thinly sliced top round)

8 cups (2 L) water

1 tsp. (5 mL) salt

- In a large soup pot, combine meat, water and salt. Bring to a boil, reduce heat and simmer, uncovered and stirring occasionally, 2 hours or until meat is tender.

- Drain meat well and thinly slice with the grain; neatly fan out slices on plates.

Serve with boiled baby potatoes and a mixture of steamed root vegetables and cabbage.

SERVES 4.

Stuffed Moose Heart with Gravy

You can use the stuffing suggested in this recipe, or you can use some of the Mahekun Wild Rice Casserole (p. 78). Either way, the results are great.

    1 moose heart, 2 to 3 lb. (1 to 1.5 kg)

    1 cup (250 mL) dry or fresh bread crumbs

    1 small onion, chopped

    1 stalk celery, chopped

    ¼ cup (50 mL) unsalted butter, melted

    1 cup (250 mL) all-purpose flour

    Salt and pepper

    2 tsp. (10 mL) unsalted butter

- Soak heart overnight in unsalted water. Drain well and hollow out the top.

- In a bowl, combine bread crumbs, onion, celery and melted butter. Stuff into heart.

- In a shallow dish, mix flour, salt and pepper; roll heart in seasoned flour to coat evenly and place in a covered roasting pan. Dot with butter. Roast, uncovered, at 425°F (220°C) for 25 minutes; baste with melted butter, cover and roast at 325°F (160°C) about 2½ hours, until juices coming from the heart run clear and meat is firm to the touch.

Gravy

    3 cups (750 mL) water

    ¼ cup (50 mL) all-purpose flour

    2 cups (500 mL) cold water

    Salt and pepper

- Remove heart from pan and keep warm. Set pan over high heat and deglaze with 3 cups (750 mL) water, stirring well to scrape up any brown bits. Reduce heat.

- Whisk together flour and 2 cups (500 mL) cold water; pour into roasting pan, stirring until thickened. Remove from heat and season to taste.

Slice heart, arrange on a platter and serve with gravy.

Serves 4 to 6.

ABORIGINAL MIXED GRILL

Now here is the way to have a mixed grill. This Aboriginal version is long on flavour and lower in fat and cholesterol than other mixed grills. And it's so quick and simple, whether done under your broiler or on the barbecue.

You can get these meats in most specialty butcher shops these days.

> 4 smoked buffalo sausages, 2 oz. (50 g) each
>
> 4 venison sausages, 2 oz. (50 g) each
>
> 4 wild boar chops, 2 oz. (50 g) each

- In a large skillet, bring ½ inch (1 cm) water to a boil and blanch sausages 10 minutes. Drain well and pat dry.

- On a rack 6 inches (15 cm) from the heat, broil or barbecue chops 6 to 8 minutes on one side for rare. Turn chops, add sausages and broil or barbecue another 6 to 8 minutes, turning sausages to brown on all sides.

Serve with Wild Rice and Mushrooms (p. 77) or baked sweet potato, and eat without guilt.

SERVES 4.

Savoury Steaks
Gihl Lakh Khun

This recipe is one of my favourites. I have enjoyed it ever since I can remember. My mother, Rita, would make a big feast of savoury steaks for our family during hunting season. I've used her Hereditary Chief name, Gihl Lakh Khun, to honour her for this dish.

4 Moose steaks (or venison, veal or beef), 8 oz. (250 g) each

¼ cup (50 mL) cornstarch

1 tbsp. (15 mL) dry mustard

Salt and pepper to taste

2 tsp. (10 mL) vegetable oil

2 onions, thinly sliced

1 carrot, diced

1½ cups (375 mL) canned tomatoes, chopped

◆ Using the tip of a sharp knife, nick steaks all over to tenderize them.

◆ In a small bowl, mix cornstarch, mustard, salt and pepper. Sprinkle over steaks and pound into meat with a meat mallet.

◆ In a large skillet over high heat, heat oil. Sear steaks on both sides. Transfer to a roasting pan. Cover steaks with onions, carrot and tomatoes. Roast steaks, covered, at 375°F (190°C) for 1½ hours or until meat is tender.

Serve steaks with the vegetables and pan juices and with steamed rice or roasted potatoes.

SERVES 4.

WILD GAME MEAT LOAF

I'm using venison here but you can use any wild meat, such as moose, caribou or buffalo. (You can also use beef or veal, but that defeats the purpose, doesn't it?)

Venison is a very lean meat and needs the pork fat for moisture and to hold the loaf together.

2 lb. (1 kg) ground venison

½ lb. (250 g) ground pork back fat

1 cup (250 mL) crushed soda crackers

1 egg, lightly beaten

½ cup (125 mL) milk

1 onion, diced

½ green pepper, diced

2 tsp. (10 mL) Worcestershire sauce

Salt and pepper to taste

2 cloves garlic, crushed

- In a large bowl, combine all ingredients. Blend well, but do not overwork the meat.
- Pack the mixture into a lightly greased 9- x 5-inch (2 L) loaf pan and baked at 375°F (190°C) for 45 minutes.

Serve with mashed potatoes and mixed seasonal vegetables.

SERVES 4.

WILD RABBIT SOUP

Like all of our soups, this one goes well with hot bannock. Cruise the bannock section of Feast! *and choose the type you want to enjoy with a bowl of steaming hot wild rabbit soup.*

People from Europe seem to prefer hare to rabbit. I don't know about you, but I've never liked hare in my soup.

1 wild rabbit, cut into eight pieces

1 medium onion, diced

1 stalk celery, diced

3 slices of bacon, diced

Salt and pepper to taste

1½ cups (375 mL) white rice

8 cups (2 L) cold water

- Place rabbit, onion, celery and bacon in a large soup pot and cover with water. Boil, stirring occasionally, 30 minutes.

- Stir in rice; reduce heat and simmer until rice is tender, about 25 minutes. Adjust seasoning.

SERVES 4.

Rabbit Stew

This is thicker and heartier than the wild rabbit soup, and every bit as tasty.

1 rabbit (2 to 3 lb./1 to 1.5 kg), cut into eight pieces

2 stalks celery, diced

1 large onion, diced

1 bay leaf

¼ tsp. (1 mL) thyme

1 tbsp. (15 mL) each salt and pepper

6 cups (1.5 L) water

2 carrots, diced

1 large russet potato, diced

2 tbsp. (25 mL) all-purpose flour

¾ cup (175 mL) cold water

- Place rabbit in a large soup pot with celery, onion, bay leaf, thyme, salt, pepper and 6 cups (1.5 L) water; bring to a boil, reduce heat and simmer, uncovered and without stirring, 2 hours.

- Add carrots and potato. Simmer until vegetables are tender, about 20 minutes.

- Whisk together flour and ¾ cup (175 mL) cold water; stir into stew and cook, stirring, until stew is thickened. Adjust seasoning.

SERVES 4.

PAN-FRIED RABBIT WITH WILD CRANBERRY GLAZE

*T*he glaze is what sets this dish apart. What a wonderful gourmet meal to serve to company, or just to enjoy yourself.

> 2 cups (500 mL) wild cranberries
>
> 1 cup (250 mL) sugar
>
> 1 cup (250 mL) water
>
> 2 tbsp. (25 mL) bacon fat
>
> 1 cup (250 mL) all-purpose flour
>
> Salt and pepper to taste
>
> 1 rabbit (3 to 4 lb./1.5 to 2 kg)
> (or two 2 lb./1 kg rabbits), cut into eight pieces

- In a small saucepan, bring cranberries, sugar and water to a boil, stirring; reduce heat and simmer until glaze thickens, about 30 minutes. Set aside.

- In a large cast-iron skillet over medium-high heat, melt bacon fat. Meanwhile, in a bowl, mix flour, salt and pepper. Dredge rabbit in seasoned flour and shake off excess.

- Brown rabbit in skillet and transfer skillet to a 375°F (190°C) oven 15 to 25 minutes or until rabbit is firm to the touch but tender. Pour glaze over rabbit and roast another 5 minutes.

Serve with wild rice and Fiddleheads Wabanaki (p. 75).

SERVES 4.

BOILED PORCUPINE

Preparing porcupine was taught to me by my father, Tsaibesa. He says this method was used a lot by trappers out on the land. Not too many people do it any more, but I want to share with you the old way of preparing food for survival.

They would skewer the porcupine on a big stick and hold it over a campfire to scorch off the quills. Then they would scrape and clean the carcass and cut it into small pieces for boiling.

Here's another method.

> 1 porcupine, dressed, cut into eighths
>
> 1 onion, diced
>
> 2 stalks celery, diced
>
> 3 large potatoes, chopped
>
> ½ tsp. (2 mL) salt
>
> 4–6 cups water

- In large pot, bring water to a boil.
- Add ingredients, bring to boil again.
- Reduce heat and simmer for 1½ hours.

Serve with hot bannock.

SERVES 4-6.

SMOKED BEAVER MEAT

Beaver meat has a taste I would describe as a cross between beef and the dark meat of a turkey. This method of smoking beaver meat was taught to me by my mother. It has an excellent rich flavour.

1 beaver

- Skin a gutted beaver and cut off the head and tail. (The tail can be smoked or frozen for later use.)

- Using a sharp knife, cut along the backbone from the neck to the tail. Lay the beaver on one side and, using the rib cage as a guide, cut the meat away from the ribs (like boning a chicken breast). Repeat on the other side.

- Remove the legs.

- Prepare the smoke house or smoker unit with cottonwood or alder; rotten wood works even better because the fire smoulders a long time with no real heat.

- Smoke the carcass 2 to 3 days, depending how dry you want the meat.

SERVES UP TO **10** VERY HUNGRY PEOPLE.

Boiled Smoked Beaver

Boiling the meat makes it moister and even more tender.

2 lb. (1 kg) smoked beaver

1 tsp. (5 mL) salt

◆ Place beaver and salt in a large heavy saucepan with enough water to cover. Bring to a boil, reduce heat and simmer, uncovered and without stirring, 2 to 2½ hours, or until meat is tender.

Drain meat well and serve with boiled potatoes and steamed root vegetables.

SERVES 4.

BRAISED BEAR

Roasting bear meat is the best way to keep it juicy. It may be cooked the same as pork, roasting 20 minutes per pound (500 g) at 375°F (190°C).

1 leg of young bear, 3 to 4 lb. (1.5 to 2 kg)

½ cup (125 mL) red wine or malt vinegar

½ cup (125 mL) white or rosé wine

Salt and pepper to taste

½ tsp. (2 mL) thyme

½ tsp. (2 mL) marjoram

¼ tsp. (1 mL) allspice

1 clove garlic, crushed

- Wipe roast with paper towels and put in a baking dish with vinegar and wine, turning to coat meat evenly. Cover and refrigerate at least 3 hours, turning meat occasionally.

- In a small bowl, mix salt, pepper, thyme, marjoram, allspice and garlic.

- Remove meat from marinade; reserve marinade. Pat meat dry and rub seasoning mixture all over meat.

- In a dutch oven over medium-high heat, sear meat until well-browned on all sides. Add reserved marinade, stirring to scrape up any brown bits. Simmer, covered, 3 to 4 hours until meat is very tender.

Serve sliced bear with pan juices.

SERVES 6 TO 8.

Bear Steaks

Use young, tender bear. Venison steaks can be cooked the same way.

4 bear steaks 6 to 8 oz. (175 to 250 g) each

1 large onion, thinly sliced

Unsalted butter

Salt and pepper to taste

- Rub steaks generously with butter. Sprinkle with salt and pepper.
- On a rack 6 inches (15 cm) from the heat, broil steaks 8 to 10 minutes on one side. Turn. Arrange onions on uncooked side of steaks, dot generously with butter. Broil 8 to 10 minutes.

Serves 4.

FROM
THE
SKIES

*T*he eagle and the hawk soar high on thermal columns, circling in search of their prey in the valleys and canyons of Now'h Yin'h Ta'h. Below, the air is abuzz with activity — birds and butterflies and other insects constantly and noisily on the move. In autumn and spring the skies are heavily speckled with Canada geese and other migrating species. Sudden noise makes the partridge and grouse flutter from forest floor to treetop, and back again in search of food when the danger has passed.

The skies are busy with life, as are the waters, the earth and the land in Wet'suwet'en territory.

Andrew and his family often look to the skies as a provider. When they do, there are wonderful dishes they prepare to grace the table. Recipes for some of them are shared with you in "From the Skies."

DUCK STOCK

For use in all kinds of soups and sauces, such as Wild Duck and Winter Vegetable Soup (p. 147) or the sauce for Toody Ni Juniper Duck (p. 149).

> 4 lb. (2 kg) duck bones, preferably wild
>
> 5 qt. (5 L) cold water
>
> 2 carrots, diced
>
> 2 stalks celery, diced
>
> 1 onion, diced
>
> 1 bouquet garni, made with 1 bay leaf,
> ½ tsp./2 mL thyme, ½ tsp./2 mL oregano)

- ◆ In a large soup pot, bring bones and water to a simmer.

- ◆ Add carrots, celery, onion and bouquet garni. Return to a simmer. Skim foam off top.

- ◆ Simmer, uncovered and skimming occasionally, 3 hours. Strain stock through a fine sieve. Stock will keep, refrigerated, one week if brought to the boil every two days, or may be frozen.

MAKES 3½ TO 4 QT. (3.5 TO 4 L).

WILD FOWL STOCK

This is my Wet'suwet'en version of chicken stock. Of course you can make it as a chicken stock, but prairie chicken, grouse and partridge are a little closer to my heart.

> 4 lb. (2 kg) wild fowl bones
>
> 4 carrots, diced
>
> 4 onions, diced
>
> 4 stalks celery, diced
>
> 2 tbsp. (25 mL) tomato paste
>
> 1 sprig fresh thyme
>
> 1 bay leaf
>
> 5 qt. (5 L) cold water

- Place bones, carrots, onions, celery, mushrooms, tomato paste, thyme and bay leaf in a roasting pan and roast at 350°F (180°C) for 1 to 1½ hours, stirring occasionally.

- Transfer bones and vegetables to a large soup pot, add water and bring to a boil. Skim foam from surface. Reduce heat to low and simmer stock, uncovered and without stirring, 4 to 4½ hours, skimming occasionally.

- Strain stock through a fine sieve. Stock will keep, refrigerated, for one week if brought to a boil every two days, or may be frozen.

MAKES 3½ TO 4 QT. (3.5 TO 4 L).

WILD GROUSE SOUP

The grouse is the smaller wild cousin of the domestic chicken. A good substitute is Cornish game hen.

On a cold, crisp autumn day when the leaves are red and gold and the fireplace is crackling and radiating its comforting warmth throughout the house, just imagine what a bowl of this soup would taste like, with hot bannock, of course.

Come to think of it, there's no need to imagine, is there? Soup doesn't get much simpler to make than this, and the flavour is wonderful.

2 grouse, 1½ lb. (750 g) each, cut into bite-sized pieces

6 slices bacon, diced

1 medium onion, diced

1 bay leaf

Salt and pepper to taste

8 cups (2 L) cold water

½ cup (125 mL) white rice

- In a large soup pot, combine grouse, bacon, onion, bay leaf, salt, pepper and water. Bring to a boil, reduce heat and simmer, uncovered, for 45 minutes.

- Stir in rice; simmer another 30 minutes or until rice is tender. Adjust seasoning. Discard bay leaf.

SERVES 8 TO 10.

WILD DUCK AND WINTER VEGETABLE SOUP

This soup was easy to make out in the territory in the winter. Duck is available until early winter, and the root vegetables usually last through the winter.

Can you guess what we serve this soup with? It is also very good with hot buttered French bread.

¼ cup (50 mL) unsalted butter

1 medium carrot, diced

1 large russet or new potato, diced

1 small turnip, diced

2 leeks, white part only, diced

½ onion, diced

¼ cabbage, thinly sliced

8 cups (2 L) duck stock (p. 156)

1 bouquet garni, made with ¼ tsp. (1 mL) each thyme, oregano and parsley, and 1 bay leaf

30 peppercorns, crushed

1 lb. (500 g) wild duck, cut in thin strips

Salt and pepper to taste

- In a large saucepan over medium heat, melt butter. Add carrot, potato, turnip, leek, onion and cabbage; cook, stirring occasionally, until onions are transparent.

- Add stock; bring to a simmer. Add bouquet garni, peppercorns and duck; simmer, uncovered and stirring occasionally, 45 minutes.

- Season with salt and additional pepper.

SERVES 6 TO 8.

STUFFED WILD DUCK

You can use domestic duck for this recipe, of course, although I find wild duck is so much tastier and lower in fat.

1 wild duck, 4 to 5 lb. (2 to 2.2 kg)

2 cups (500 mL) dry bread crumbs

1 apple, diced

1 onion, diced

1 stalk celery, diced

½ cup (125 mL) bacon fat, melted

¼ tsp. (1 mL) sage

¼ tsp. (1 mL) thyme

Salt and pepper to taste

½ cup (125 mL) duck or chicken stock

¼ cup (50 mL) juniper berries, roughly crushed

¼ cup (50 mL) all-purpose flour

½ cup (125 mL) cold water

- Trim visible fat from duck.

- In a large bowl, mix together bread crumbs, onion, apple, celery, bacon fat, sage, thyme, salt and pepper. Stuff into duck and place duck on a rack in a roasting pan.

- Roast at 425°F (220°C) for 45 to 50 minutes, basting several times. To check for doneness, squeeze a drumstick between your fingers — it should be firm. Transfer duck to a cutting board and keep warm.

- Pour off excess fat and set pan over high heat. Deglaze with stock, stirring to scrape up any brown bits. Stir in juniper berries. Whisk together flour and water; stir into sauce until thickened. Remove from heat.

Carve duck into serving pieces and arrange on plates with some of the stuffing. Pour sauce over duck.

SERVES 4.

Toody Ni Juniper Duck

This is a great favourite of anyone I prepare it for. The recipe is quite simple, and the end product is spectacular. Think of it: smoked duck breast, and red wine, and juniper berries. Use your imagination as you read this recipe and the flavours will almost jump off the pages onto your palate, even before you start cooking.

2 boneless smoked duck breasts

Salt and pepper to taste

2 tsp. (10 mL) vegetable oil

1 large shallot, chopped

1 tbsp. (15 mL) juniper berries, crushed

⅓ cup (75 mL) red wine

½ cup (125 mL) duck stock or demi-glace

- Season duck with salt and pepper and place skin side up on a rack in a broiling pan.

- In a small saucepan over medium-high heat, heat oil. Sauté shallots and juniper berries until shallots are transparent. Add wine and stock and boil until reduced by half. Pour sauce over duck and broil 6 inches (15 cm) from the heat for 5 minutes. Baste breasts with sauce and roast at 375°F (190°C) for 10 minutes or until breast is firm to the touch and juices run clear. Arrange breasts on plates and spoon sauce over them.

Serve with Fiddleheads Wabanaki (p. 75) and Baked Sweet Potato with Roasted Hazelnuts (p. 80).

SERVES 2.

GAME HEN WITH MANY STUFFINGS

*F*or the stuffing in this recipe, you have three choices. Whichever you choose, you won't be disappointed.

> 4 Cornish game hens
>
> 1½ cups (375 mL) Stuffing for Game Birds (p. 90)
> *or* Wild Rice and Mushrooms (p. 77)
> *or* Mahekun Wild Rice Casserole (p. 78)
>
> 2 tbsp. (25 mL) vegetable oil
>
> Salt and pepper to taste
>
> 3 tbsp. (50 mL) chicken stock
>
> Chopped fresh parsley, for garnish
>
> 4 sprigs watercress, for garnish

◆ Debone game hens, remove drumsticks and reshape to original form. Fill cavities with stuffing. Brush hens with oil, season with salt and pepper and place on a rack in a roasting pan. Roast at 400°F (200°C) for 20 to 30 minutes or until meat is brown. Remove hens from pan and keep warm.

◆ Pour off excess fat from pan, set pan over high heat and pour in chicken stock, stirring to scrape up any brown bits. Reduce heat and simmer 5 minutes; season and strain if desired.

◆ Arrange hens on plates, spoon sauce over them.

Serve with a mixture of root vegetables or fiddleheads.

SERVES 4.

ROAST GOOSE

If you follow this recipe properly, your goose will be cooked. And you will enjoy its taste too, especially if it's Canada goose.

> ¼ cup (50 mL) unsalted butter, melted
>
> 1 onion, chopped
>
> ½ cup (125 mL) chopped celery
>
> 1 cup (250 mL) dry bread crumbs
>
> ½ cup (125 mL) milk
>
> 1 cup (250 mL) mashed potatoes
>
> 1 tbsp. (15 mL) sage
>
> Salt and pepper to taste
>
> 1 goose, 4 to 5 lb. (2 to 2.2 kg)

- In a large skillet over medium heat, heat 2 tsp. (10 mL) of the melted butter. Fry onion and celery until tender. Mix in bread crumbs and milk. Remove from heat. Stir in potatoes, remaining melted butter, sage, salt and pepper. Stuff mixture into goose.

- Place goose on a rack in a covered roasting pan and roast, covered, at 350°F (180°C) for 2 hours. Uncover goose and roast, basting occasionally, about another 30 minutes or until meat is firm.

Serve with mixed root vegetables and Baked Sweet Potato with Roasted Hazelnuts (p. 80).

SERVES 4 TO 6.

STUFFED WILD GOOSE WITH APPLES

Imagine the great smells in the kitchen as the goose, the apples, the cinnamon and the bacon join forces in the oven. It's too bad we can't all do this one in my Tsaibesa's old wood stove.

1 goose, 4 lb. (2 kg)

10 Granny Smith apples

2 tbsp. (25 mL) sugar

1 tsp. (5 mL) cinnamon

Salt and pepper to taste

Fat

4 slices bacon

- Trim goose of visible fat.

- Chop apples into bite-sized pieces and, in a bowl, mix well with sugar.

- Season goose with salt and pepper. In a large deep skillet over medium-high heat, heat fat. Sear goose on all sides. Transfer goose to a rack in a roasting pan and stuff cavity with half the apple mixture. Top goose with bacon strips and the rest of the apples. Roast at 375°F (190°C) for 50 to 60 minutes or until leg is firm to the touch and skin at end of leg pulls away from the bone.

Serve with Wild Rice and Mushrooms (p. 77) and steamed dilled baby carrots.

SERVES 4.

Pan-fried Wild Ptarmigan (Mountain Hen)

So many foods taste terrific when cooked in a cast-iron pan. This is one of them.

4 slices bacon

½ cup (125 mL) all-purpose flour

Salt and pepper to taste

2 ptarmigan or grouse, 1½ lb. (750 g) each,
cut into bite-sized pieces

- In a large cast-iron skillet over medium heat, fry bacon until crisp. Drain bacon on paper towels and keep warm. Set skillet aside.

- In a small bowl, mix flour, salt and pepper. Dredge ptarmigan in seasoned flour, shaking off excess.

- Fry ptarmigan in the bacon fat over medium-high heat, 8 to 10 minutes each side or until meat pulls away from bone easily. Serve ptarmigan topped with bacon.

Serve with wild rice and vegetables.

SERVES 4.

PROP CREDITS

SPIRIT BRAID SEAFOOD PLATTER
plate and cutlery: Presents of Mind

FEAST! SEAFOOD SPREAD
bowls and platter: Chintz & Co.

BAKED SWEET POTATO WITH ROASTED HAZELNUTS
ladle: Leona Lattimer • *nut bowl:* Country Furniture • *chair:* Folkart

SALMON SOUP WETSU'WET'EN
glass: Country Furniture • *bowl:* Presents of Mind

PACIFIC SALMON AND ATLANTIC FIDDLEHEAD STIR-FRY
vase: Motiv • *plate:* Presents of Mind

SEAFOOD CHOWDER TOODY NI
bowl: Kaya Kaya

SMOKED SALMON ON BANNOCK FINGERS
plate: Presents of Mind

TSAIBESA'S BANNOCK
background and metal grill: Folkart

FRESH WILD BERRIES TOPPED WITH SOAPALILLIE
glasses: Chintz & Co.

WILD FLOWER SALAD
glass bowl: Kaya Kaya

FIDDLEHEADS WABANAKI
plate: Presents of Mind

MOOSE OR BUFFALO STEW WITH DUMPLINGS
background and wooden spoons: Forest Hill Antiques
cast iron: Folkart • *basket:* Uno Langmann Ltd.

ABORIGINAL MIXED GRILL
no credits

PAN-FRIED RABBIT WITH WILD CRANBERRY GLAZE
glass: Country Furniture • *plate:* Lightheart & Co. • *cutlery:* Motiv

GAME HEN WITH WILD RICE
plate: Motiv • *fabric:* Chintz & Co.

INDEX